CULTURALLY RESPONSIVE
DESIGN
FOR ENGLISH LEARNERS

THE UDL APPROACH

Patti Kelly Ralabate, EdD • Loui Lord Nelson, PhD

CAST Professional Publishing
UNTIL LEARNING HAS NO LIMITS™

Library of Congress Control Number: 2017944060
Paperback ISBN 978-1-930583-05-4
Ebook ISBN 978-1-930583-06-1

Published by:

CAST Professional Publishing
an imprint of CAST, Inc.
Wakefield, Massachusetts, USA

For information about special discounts for bulk purchases, please email *publishing@cast.org* or telephone 781-245-2212 or visit *www.castpublishing.org*

Cover and interior design by Happenstance Type-O-Rama
Illustrations by Eli Brophy

Printed in the United States of America

CONTENTS

FIGURES AND TABLES

CHAPTER 1

CHAPTER 2

CHAPTER 3

CHAPTER 4

CHAPTER 5

CHAPTER 6

CHAPTER 7

CHAPTER 8

CHAPTER 9

ACKNOWLEDGMENTS

We jointly express our appreciation to CAST Professional Publishing for offering us the opportunity to write this book. In particular, we want to acknowledge David Gordon for his adept guidance and Billie Fitzpatrick and Liz Welch for their editing expertise. In addition, we want to thank Eli Brophy for providing his fantastic, artistic illustrations.

FROM PATTI RALABATE: I'm delighted to have had the opportunity to create this book with my friend and co-author, Dr. Loui Lord Nelson. You made it fun and easy! I'm grateful to Dr. Christine Magee of The George Washington University's Graduate School of Education and Human Development for the opportunity to teach in their unique Special Education for Culturally and Linguistically Diverse Learners program. Many of the real examples in the book come from working with these fabulous GW students whose dedication to their diverse students is unwavering: thank you for enriching our learning. Lastly, I want to express my deep gratitude to my husband Sam and daughter Kelly for your enduring patience and support. You continue to be the wind beneath my wings.

FROM LOUI LORD NELSON: Co-authoring this book with Dr. Patti Ralabate took me back to our collaborative planning and writing while we worked together at CAST. Just as in the past, I benefited from your energy and passion as it flowed onto these pages each day. It was invigorating to "bump into" you while working in our digitally based collaborative space and then catching up during our scheduled calls. Our system kept us honest and on track! Scenarios and stories were heavily influenced by my former middle school students and the time I spent as a teaching assistant in a high school English learners' language lab. I am indebted to those students and partner teachers. This book also gave me the opportunity to reflect on the students', teachers', and my own experiences and ask, "How can I help educators design fully accessible learning environments for all students?" Bill Jensen at Bartholomew Consolidated School Corporation in Columbus, IN, pushed me to write this book after I led a session at BCSC connecting UDL and Culturally Responsive Teaching in 2015. Here's to your tenacity, Bill. Finally, I thank my parents Bill and Cathy and my sister Jennifer for your daily support via email, phone calls, and meals. And thanks to my husband Carl. You remind me every day that all things are possible.

INTRODUCTION

As classrooms become more culturally and linguistically diverse, educators need to know how to meet the diverse learning needs of all students. Many teachers are seeking ways to welcome every learner into engaging, meaningful, culturally responsive learning environments. You are likely one of those teachers. We wrote this book to help you and teachers like you to weave together two powerful frameworks—Universal Design for Learning (UDL) and Culturally Responsive Teaching (CRT)—to design culturally responsive learning environments and lesson plans to meet the needs of English learners (ELs).

We met at one of the first national conferences focused on UDL and were thrilled to meet others who were as passionate about UDL and inclusive practice as we were! Within a year, we were neighbors, both working at CAST, researching UDL implementation and developing professional development programs for teachers and administrators who were willing to change their practice in an effort to better meet learners' needs. This book is a natural outgrowth of our work with educators across the United States and in many parts of the world who share our joint vision of inclusive practice. Because our teaching histories are rooted in the classroom, we found our perspectives to be razor-focused on bringing the theories of UDL and CRT to life in ways that you can use immediately.

WHY FOCUS ON BOTH UDL AND CRT?

The braiding of UDL and CRT is a natural extension of the ethos of both frameworks: both UDL and CRT recognize and respect variability among learners. The research on social and cultural theory affirms that each person is raised in at least one culture, that each cultural experience impacts learning in a unique way, and that learners glean their background knowledge and social capital via their culture (Orosco & O'Connor, 2011; Vygotsky 1962, 1978; Waitoller & Thorius, 2016). Similarly, neuroscience research asserts that every person learns differently, that learning is based on context, and that learning can be enhanced by strategies that address learner variability (Meyer, Rose, & Gordon, 2014). In addition, research on linguistic skills shows that language acquisition needs among ELs are best met in an environment that builds on learners' prior learning and provides them with opportunities to construct new pathways of learning (Haynes, n.d.; Hill & Miller, 2013). Because we know learners come from a variety of cultures, we turn to Culturally Responsive Teaching and UDL to design successful learning environments to meet the needs of all learners.

To provide a lens that any educator can use to enhance his or her practice, this book aims to establish a bridge between UDL and CRT, with particular attention to the language needs of ELs. Although lots of educators are familiar with UDL, others are not. Many are knowledgeable about Culturally Responsive Teaching pedagogy; some are not. A core group of teachers are familiar with teaching strategies for ELs; most are not. This book focuses on how to apply the UDL and CRT frameworks to (1) design culturally responsive instruction for all learners and (2) address language learning needs for English learners (ELs) specifically.

The book is divided into two parts:

Part I lays a foundation for understanding Culturally Responsive Design by exploring how culture and language shape learning, explaining critical aspects of variability and culture (chapters 1 and 2). Chapter 3 crosswalks the three principles of UDL and seven principles of CRT proposed by Brown University. This is followed by a deeper discussion of Culturally Responsive Teaching in chapter 4.

In this part, readers will learn the following:

- *How UDL applies to learner variability among CLD students.* Chapter 2 explores the concept of learner variability and its implications for planning for diverse classrooms.

- *How native or first-language culture and language impacts learning.* Chapter 2 explains evidence regarding how culture shapes learning.

- *How to apply Culturally Responsive Teaching (CRT) strategies to UDL-infused learning environments.* Chapter 3 delves into an explanation of the principles of CRT (as proposed by Brown University, 2017), and chapter 4 focuses on identifying potential barriers to CRT, with suggestions on how to use UDL.

Part II describes typical stages of second- or dual-language learning and focuses on how UDL and CRT strategies bolster language acquisition for ELs. Although all three UDL principles are important, we've chosen to highlight the principle of Action and Expression first (chapter 5)—dealing with language expression and planning strategies—because of its significance in the second- or dual-language development process. Chapters 6 and 7 explain intersections between various frameworks (e.g., WIDA and SIOP/SEI) and their application to effective instruction for ELs. Chapter 8 illustrates culturally responsive lesson planning through the perspective of a school team that is applying both UDL and CRT to their teaching. As a final enhancement, the last chapter serves as a resource on important federal policy for U.S. educators who are interested in advocating for appropriate, inclusive services for students with disabilities and ELs.

In this part, readers will learn the following:

- *How to integrate UDL with traditional English as a second language (ESL) approaches.* Chapter 5 connects UDL with traditional second- and dual-language teaching strategies.

- *How to apply the UDL principles infused with CRT to meet the learning needs of culturally and linguistically diverse learners, specifically ELs.* Chapters 5, 6, and 7 outline strategies specifically addressing the strategic, recognition, and affective networks.

- *How to infuse the UDL framework into lesson planning for ELs.* Chapter 8 presents ideas for UDL lesson planning that is responsive to the learning needs of CLD students.

- *How U.S. policy impacts instruction for students with special needs.* The final chapter reviews key federal statutes and court rulings that define the civil and educational rights of learners.

We recognize that CRT is a complex topic and heavily charged. Being culturally responsive means taking a close look at how we interact with people of different cultures, including our students. It is a self-investigative process that leads to changes in our practice, but those changes aren't always easy. Being culturally responsive makes us reflect on our thoughts and actions, both conscious and subconscious, that might have made our former students feel uncomfortable, frustrated, or detached from learning. No teacher wants that for his or her students, and it's easy to go down the road of discouragement, anger, and some confusion. While that discomfort is part of becoming more aware (Gay, 2010; Tatum, 1997), we encourage educators to continue taking the steps suggested in this book, and by others referenced, so you can use your new knowledge to inform the design of future, culturally responsive learning environments. We come to this from the perspective of UDL—how educators can use the UDL framework to apply CRT practices to benefit all students.

In an effort to "walk the talk," this book models the UDL principles through scenarios, summaries, multiple illustrations, reflection questions, and application exercises as it guides educators in creating UDL-infused, culturally responsive lessons. Each chapter includes an exercise you can use to check your understanding before you move ahead. If you want to delve into specific concepts, see the web-based resources spotlighted throughout the book and the extensive list of references. Ultimately, the aim of this book is to assist you in becoming an expert at culturally responsive UDL design for all learners.

PART I

A Foundation for Culturally Responsive Design:
How Culture, Context, and Language Shape Learning

1

Culturally Responsive Design Matters

This chapter offers an overview of Universal Design for Learning (UDL) and Culturally Responsive Teaching (CRT). We also present a rationale for *Culturally Responsive Design*, including planning learning environments and instruction for culturally and linguistically diverse (CLD) students and English learners (ELs), and we describe expert learning and expert teachers.

● Meet Felicia

"Oh, boy!" Felicia, a 9th-grade biology teacher, remarks as she reviews her class list with her colleague Allyssa, a 10th-grade geometry teacher. "I don't know how I'm going to do it this year. So many of my students are English learners and they come from all over. I don't even know how to pronounce many of the names on my class list."

Allyssa jumps in, "I've been using Culturally Responsive Teaching strategies for years, but this year, I'm also going to integrate UDL—Universal Design for Learning."

"I thought UDL was just for students with disabilities," Felicia counters.

"That's a common misconception about UDL," explains Allyssa. "The UDL framework focuses on how we all learn, which includes the cultural variability and language learning needs of English learners."

"That's just what I need!" declares Felicia. "I'm going to look into UDL."

REFLECTION How do Felicia's concerns relate to your beliefs about your own instruction?

CULTURAL AND LINGUISTIC DIVERSITY AND UDL

Felicia's situation is a common one. She is deeply devoted to her teaching, but as her school's student population changes, she finds it more difficult to meet their diverse learning needs. She's heard about Universal Design for Learning (UDL) but has mistakenly believed that it is only helpful for students with disabilities. That's a frequent misunderstanding. As Allyssa asserts, UDL helps educators to address the learning needs of all students, including those who are English learners (ELs).

According to the 2013 U.S. Census, almost 21 percent of people over the age of five speak at least one language other than English (U.S. Census, 2013). As classrooms in the United States become more culturally and linguistically diverse, educators are under pressure to meet the learning needs of ELs without diluting the focus of their educational goals and curriculum, and potentially sacrificing the progress of other students. The good news is that there is a framework they can apply to their lesson planning to reach all learners: Universal Design for Learning (UDL). UDL offers a unique lesson planning process that helps educators to develop learning environments that respond culturally and proactively to the needs of all learners, including culturally and linguistically diverse (CLD) students and English learners (Chita-Tegmark, Gravel, Serpa, Domings, & Rose, 2012).

The UDL framework is defined in the Higher Education Opportunity Act (HEOA) of 2008 as "a scientifically valid framework for guiding educational practice" for all students, "including students with disabilities and students who are limited English proficient" (see 122 Stat. 3088). Based on learning and cognitive neuroscience research, UDL espouses a set of principles, illustrated in figure 1.1, that drive curriculum and learning environment design. The three UDL principles address specific sets of neural networks and are used by educators to engage learners in learning (i.e., Engagement, addressing the Affective networks), represent accessible and meaningful information (i.e., Representation, addressing with the Recognition networks), and offer options for expressing their learning (i.e., Action and Expression, addressing the Strategic networks).

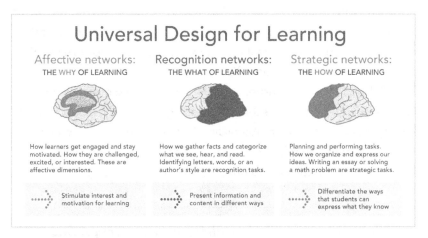

FIGURE 1.1: The three UDL principles © CAST (2014). USED WITH PERMISSION

A key premise of UDL—that curricula should be designed from the outset with built-in flexibility and choice—requires some educators to make a conceptual shift from traditional ways of thinking about lesson design, curriculum, and learners. Educators who use the UDL framework understand that an inflexible, one-size-fits-all curriculum creates barriers that prevent students from reaching learning goals. Rather than expecting learners to access concepts, express their learning, and engage with assessments, materials, and methods in only one way, teachers who apply UDL to their teaching design flexible instruction with multiple options and choices (Meyer, Rose, & Gordon, 2014). Concisely stated, "UDL is a framework that guides the shift from designing learning environments and lessons with potential barriers to designing barrier-free, instructionally rich learning environments and lessons" (Nelson, 2014, p. 2).

CULTURALLY RESPONSIVE TEACHING

Another common framework for addressing the learning needs of CLD students and ELs that aligns well with UDL is Culturally Responsive Teaching (CRT). Geneva Gay, a pioneer in the field, defines Culturally Responsive Teaching as "using the cultural knowledge, prior experiences, frames of reference, and performance styles of ethnically diverse students to make learning encounters more relevant to and effective for them" (Gay, 2010, p. 31).

CRT builds on the learner's culture. What do we mean by culture? Culture is not limited to ethnic or racial groups. Any group or community possesses *culture*. According to Ung (2015), culture includes a group's, community's, or society's shared beliefs, values, norms, expectations, practices, and unspoken rules of conduct.

Culture is not limited to ethnic or racial groups. Any group or community possesses culture.

CRT involves valuing, building on, and teaching from each learner's experiences and background knowledge gained through his own interactions within his culture. Gay (2010) doesn't stop there, though. She reminds us that CRT is not just how we design our lessons or structure the environment; CRT is how we acknowledge the importance of cultural diversity in learning. When we understand the value of diversity, we begin to celebrate and "empower students intellectually, socially, emotionally, and politically by using cultural referents to impart knowledge, skills, and attitudes" (Ladson-Billings, 2001, p. 17–18).

EXPERT LEARNERS AND EXPERT TEACHERS

Helping students become expert learners is one of the primary goals of applying UDL to teaching practice. Frankly, no matter what their background, all students can become expert learners. Expert learners are not necessarily the most academically or linguistically proficient students in the classroom. Instead, expert learners are motivated and capable of managing their learning by focusing on a goal and identifying ways to reach that goal. They might not know all of the needed strategies when they begin working toward a goal, but they are resourceful about finding or using new strategies. In a nutshell, Meyer, Rose, & Gordon (2014) define expert learners as resourceful, knowledgeable, strategic, goal directed, and purposeful.

Essentially, the process of integrating UDL with the CRT framework depends on your ability, as an expert learner, to (a) find out what you need to know, (b) acquire the desired knowledge, skills, and attitudes, and then (3) use your new knowledge effectively (Nuri-Robins, Lindsey, Lindsey, & Terrell, 2012).

Together, UDL and CRT create a foundation for creating inclusive instruction and designing learning environments that heighten engagement, clarify academic content and language concepts, and offer meaningful and relevant expression options that help all learners become expert learners.

As you learn more about UDL and CRT, keep in mind these two points: (1) successful instructional change is dependent on first determining that a change in practice is needed, and (2) successfully changing your practice to include UDL and CRT may require a conceptual shift in your existing ideas and beliefs.

PURPOSEFUL & MOTIVATED LEARNERS	RESOURCEFUL & KNOWLEDGEABLE LEARNERS	STRATEGIC & GOAL-DIRECTED LEARNERS
+ Are eager for new learning and are motivated by the mastery of learning itself	+ Bring considerable prior knowledge to new learning	+ Formulate plans for learning
+ Are goal-directed in their learning	+ Activate that prior knowledge to identify, organize, prioritize, and assimilate new information	+ Devised effective strategies and tactics to optimize learning
+ Know how to set challenging learning goals for themselves	+ Recognize the tools and resources that would help them find, structure and remember new information	+ Organize resources and tools to facilitate learning
+ Know how to sustain the effort and resilience that reaching those goals will require	+ Know how to transform new information into meaningful and useable knowledge	+ Monitor their progress
+ Monitor and regulate emotional reactions that would be impediments or distractions to their successful learning		+ Recognize their own strengths and weaknesses as learners
		+ Abandon plans and strategies that are ineffective

FIGURE 1.2: Expert learning chart © CAST, 2014. USED WITH PERMISSION.

Let's be clear: Although you may want to improve your teaching effectiveness, you may also feel that improving student performance is beyond your immediate control. Research suggests otherwise. Although students' backgrounds and abilities, home environment, school climate, school resources, and peer behaviors can impact learning, research reveals that the greatest influence on student success is the teacher (Hattie, 2003). In fact, *expert* teachers have the most direct impact on student outcomes.

Any teacher—whether a novice or experienced educator—can become an expert teacher. What is an expert teacher? Importantly, expert teachers focus on more than achievement goals and do more than cover the curriculum. Expert teachers "...engage students in learning and develop in their students' self-regulation, involvement in mastery learning, enhanced self-efficacy, and self-esteem as learners" (Hattie, 2003, p. 9). They aim to improve student self-concept, set appropriate challenging goals, and build deep understanding. Furthermore, Hattie (2003) states that expert teachers:

- Identify essential representations of their content

- Guide learning through classroom interactions

- Monitor learning and provide feedback

- Attend to affective learner needs

- Influence student outcomes (adapted from p. 5)

The exchange between Felicia and Allyssa encapsulates a number of the attributes of expert teaching. Felicia is interested in finding a way to better meet her learners' needs, particularly the ELs. Her intentions may lead her to redesign her instruction and eventually become an expert teacher. Clearly, Allyssa already has the characteristics of an expert teacher. Her plan to blend UDL and CRT illustrates that she intends to design instruction that engages learners in mastery-oriented learning, builds language and self-regulation skills, and is responsive to cultural variability.

CREATING EXPERT LEARNERS THROUGH BRAIDING CRT AND UDL

Culturally Responsive Teaching and Universal Design for Learning complement each other in today's classrooms. By applying CRT principles, you can build instruction on a value system that honors the background and culture of learners, their families, and their communities while increasing the meaning and relevancy of curriculum. By applying UDL principles (figure 1.3), you can design instruction that addresses learner variability within the classroom and honors individual learners, helping every learner become an expert learner. By braiding UDL and CRT into your practice, you are able to demonstrate essential characteristics of an expert teacher.

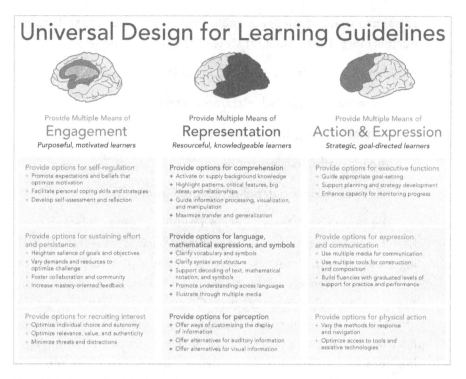

Universal Design for Learning Guidelines

Provide Multiple Means of **Engagement** *Purposeful, motivated learners*	Provide Multiple Means of **Representation** *Resourceful, knowledgeable learners*	Provide Multiple Means of **Action & Expression** *Strategic, goal-directed learners*
Provide options for self-regulation + Promote expectations and beliefs that optimize motivation + Facilitate personal coping skills and strategies + Develop self-assessment and reflection	**Provide options for comprehension** + Activate or supply background knowledge + Highlight patterns, critical features, big ideas, and relationships + Guide information processing, visualization, and manipulation + Maximize transfer and generalization	**Provide options for executive functions** + Guide appropriate goal-setting + Support planning and strategy development + Enhance capacity for monitoring progress
Provide options for sustaining effort and persistence + Heighten salience of goals and objectives + Vary demands and resources to optimize challenge + Foster collaboration and community + Increase mastery-oriented feedback	**Provide options for language, mathematical expressions, and symbols** + Clarify vocabulary and symbols + Clarify syntax and structure + Support decoding of text, mathematical notation, and symbols + Promote understanding across languages + Illustrate through multiple media	**Provide options for expression and communication** + Use multiple media for communication + Use multiple tools for construction and composition + Build fluencies with graduated levels of support for practice and performance
Provide options for recruiting interest + Optimize individual choice and autonomy + Optimize relevance, value, and authenticity + Minimize threats and distractions	**Provide options for perception** + Offer ways of customizing the display of information + Offer alternatives for auditory information + Offer alternatives for visual information	**Provide options for physical action** + Vary the methods for response and navigation + Optimize access to tools and assistive technologies

FIGURE 1.3: UDL Guidelines ©CAST, 2014. USED WITH PERMISSION.

Educators are seeking a way to plan instruction that addresses the needs of all their learners. This book, *Culturally Responsive Design for English Learners: The UDL Approach,* illustrates how to inclusively plan for all learners, including those who are CLD students and ELs. A natural relationship exists between the two frameworks that focus on meeting diverse student learning and providing culturally responsive instruction: Universal Design for Learning (UDL) and Culturally Responsive Teaching (CRT). Based on learning and cognitive neuroscience research, the UDL framework guides teachers in designing learning environments and lessons with built-in flexibility and choice. Similarly, infusing CRT in instructional design builds lessons that value, build on, and reflect each learner's experiences and background knowledge. By applying the principles of UDL and the components of CRT, expert teachers—those who focus on developing learners' self-regulation, self-efficacy, and self-esteem as well as academic success—can create responsive, inclusive classrooms that help all students, including English learners, become expert learners: learners who are resourceful, knowledgeable, strategic, goal directed, purposeful, and motivated.

REFLECTION QUESTIONS

1. In what ways does Felicia's reaction to her class list resonate with your experiences as an educator? How diverse is your class list? To what extent is the population in your school or district changing?

2. What frameworks or strategies have you used to create an inclusive learning environment? How effective have they been?

3. How satisfied are you with the responsiveness of your instruction?

4. In what ways do you prepare students to become expert learners?

5. To what extent do you feel teacher experience contributes to teacher expertise? Do you believe that applying UDL and CRT can help teachers become expert teachers?

CHECK-IN: REFLECT ON YOUR INSTRUCTIONAL DESIGN

Given what you've learned so far, how inclusive and responsive is your current instructional design? Use this matrix to evaluate the inclusive and culturally responsive aspects of your current instructional design and reflect on what components you may want to consider keeping or changing.

CHECK-IN: REFLECT ON YOUR INSTRUCTIONAL DESIGN

My instructional design addresses learning variability **and** is responsive to cultural variability.	My instructional design **does not** address learning variability **but** is responsive to cultural variability.
My instructional design addresses learning variability **but is not** responsive to cultural variability.	My instructional design **does not** address learning variability **and is not** responsive to cultural variability.

2

Learner Variability and CLD Students/ELs

This chapter reviews how the three brain networks and UDL principles are associated with cultural and linguistic variability among CLD students and ELs, the neuroscience of bilingualism, and second- or dual-language learning.

Meet Annette

Annette is a skillful third-grade teacher whose classroom is organized into learning centers. At the beginning of each school year, she traditionally identifies students by levels for the core subjects and uses those levels to define groups for each of the learning centers. This year she has enough ELs in her class to make a separate group just for them. But as the school year progresses, she confides to her colleague Lily that she's not happy with how the EL group is doing. "Why is it so difficult to plan for them?" she says. "I thought they'd have similar needs but they are almost as different in their learning as the rest of the class! Why is that?"

THE ONLY CONSTANT IS VARIABILITY

Generalizations about learners can lead to planning ineffective and unsuccessful lessons. Annette assumed that learners with one common characteristic (such as nonproficiency with English) learned in the same way. Instead, she discovered an important teaching maxim: each learner has different, unique strengths, skills, interests, desires, and readiness levels. CAST researchers state it this way: "...all individuals are unique and learn in ways that are particular to them" (Meyer, Rose, & Gordon, 2014, p. 49). Does this mean that each learner needs an individual lesson plan? Not necessarily. Recent learning and neuroscience research suggests that although similar characteristics exist among human brains, the real constant is that learning is remarkably variable (Meyer, Rose, & Gordon, 2014). Therefore, teachers need to plan with learner variability in mind.

What Do We Mean by Learner Variability?

To understand learner variability, it's helpful to delve briefly into how we learn. Although there are small specialized networks and specific parts of the typical brain that are responsible for certain functions, learning is actually accomplished through a complex system of interconnected brain networks (Meyer, Rose, & Gordon, 2014). These brain networks are made up of neurons that communicate with one another via synapses along pathways formed as individuals have experiences. Figure 2.1 shows how neural pathways multiply as an individual has different experiences.

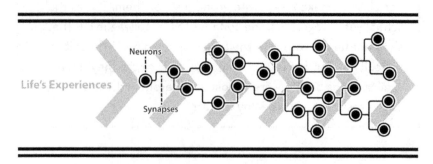

FIGURE 2.1: Experiences create neural pathways. © ELI BROPHY, PHILADELPHIA, PA

In effect, synaptic patterns are constructed every time humans experience anything. According to Hebb's theory of automaticity, as neurons fire together, they wire together—meaning that as pathways are repeatedly used, they become faster and more efficient along the pathway, leading to more automatic responses (cited in LaBerge & Samuels, 1974). For example, consider what happens when Ahmed is asked to name pictures, a frequent task for ELs (see figure 2.2). Naming a picture entails more than just verbalizing a word that matches the visual representation. A learner goes through a series of actions, such as:

- He must first perceive the visual pattern of the picture.

- Then, he must connect it with similar or other known items and meaningful experiences, including associated sensations (e.g., hearing, smell, tactile-kinesthetic).

- Next, he might invoke emotions linked to memories of personal experiences with the pictured or similar items.

- Then, he must decide which exact word matches the picture.

- Next, he must mentally formulate how to verbalize the correct vocabulary.

- And finally, he must activate and physically control the appropriate oral musculature to say the word.

FIGURE 2.2: Connections during naming tasks © ELI BROPHY, PHILADELPHIA, PA

Whew! And all of this activity happens instantaneously when Ahmed sees the picture. During an fMRI or PET scan, brain researchers see this naming task as a rapid succession of synaptic connections that light up subsections of the brain. Subtle distinctions in synaptic patterns exist for each word based on each student's learning context.

Since learning is cyclical in nature, every experience builds on previous ones. Yet because each learner responds to her learning environment with a different set of foundational experiences, students differ in how they react. What and how they learn can vary even if all learners engage in the same tasks. In effect, every brain is constantly developing as the learner's interaction with the learning environment sculpts and recasts her brain.

Planning for Learner Variability

The previous description might make planning for learner variability sound like *Mission Impossible*. The good news is that adjusting lesson plans or other curricular materials to anticipate the variability among all learners is actually easier than it sounds. Even though tremendous variability exists, neuroscience research shows that humans share a common, basic brain architecture consisting of three broad learning networks:

- **Affective** networks control how learners initiate actions and respond to the environment based on their emotions (the "why of learning").

- **Recognition** networks help learners perceive and assign meaning to information (the "what of learning").

- **Strategic** networks guide learners in planning, organizing, sequencing, coordinating, and monitoring their actions (the "how of learning"; Meyer, Rose, & Gordon, 2014).

Although each individual brain has a distinct pattern of learner variability, these three sets of networks are organized in a systematic, predictable way. The learning characteristics associated with these three learning networks are addressed by the UDL framework and outlined in the UDL Guidelines under three UDL principles:

- Provide multiple means of **Engagement** (corresponding to the Affective networks)

- Provide multiple means of **Representation** (corresponding to the Recognition networks)

- Provide multiple means of **Action and Expression** (corresponding to the Strategic networks; Meyer, Rose, & Gordon, 2014)

Educators who proactively apply the UDL principles to design curriculum and lessons are able to anticipate the variability that exists among all learners, including CLD students and ELs. Planning for learner variability in this way diminishes the need to differentiate for individual learners because the curriculum meets the needs of a wider range of learners through intentional, responsive design.

> **REFLECTION** Annette mistakenly assumed that all CLD students and ELs learn the same way and have the same learning needs. Have you noticed learner variability among the academic and learning skills of CLD students and ELs? To what extent does context or learning environment make a difference?

LANGUAGE LEARNING AND LEARNER VARIABILITY

It's essential to begin a discussion about language learning with a clear definition: language is more than the words we speak or write; language also includes nonverbal communication, such as movement of eyes, hands, and body to express information (Zion & Kozleski, 2005). In addition, language is a meaning-making process—it is how we make sense of the world around us (Halliday & Hasan, 1985). When creating lessons that are designed effectively to facilitate second- or dual-language learning and address all the different dimensions of learner variability, it is important to consider these critical points:

Context A key aspect of language learning is that it is learned within context. In other words, individuals learn language concepts as they need them for specific situations. For instance, Zoe learned food names while eating and clothing vocabulary while getting dressed. She learned how to use past tense when her teacher described events that occurred in the past and how to express hurt or joy as classmates discussed painful or happy situations. These authentic experiences offer multiple associations (e.g., engagement of senses and emotions) that stimulate the synaptic pathways in the brain needed for meaningful learning.

Connections Language evolves in a dynamic interaction that involves making connections between new features with what learners already know (i.e., prior knowledge or existing schema). Scaffolds assist learners by bridging the gap between new knowledge and prior knowledge. For example, confused by Shakespearean terms while reading *Romeo and Juliet* in his ninth-grade English class, Eli follows his teacher's suggestion to create a concept map of the story. The concept map helps him to visually link the new terms with ones he already knows. Effective scaffolds address learner variability by offering options for making meaningful connections between the new language to what the learner knows in his native or first language (L1). (For an extensive discussion of scaffolds, see chapter 5.)

DUAL- OR SECOND-LANGUAGE LEARNING

In addition to the systematic learner variability that all learners possess, varied background experiences and diverse levels of exposure to English lead to distinct dual- or second-language learning profiles. Klingner and Eppolito (2014) described four specific types of English language profiles of students:

Simultaneous Bilingual Born in the United States, Isabella has been exposed regularly but perhaps not equally to two languages since birth. In fact, most of the members of her cultural community speak Spanish, yet they often switch back and forth between English and Spanish, sometimes within the same sentence. No one in her home speaks English fluently. She's orally proficient in Spanish but never learned to read or write it.

Long-Term EL Kim was brought to the United States from Vietnam as a toddler and is now in eighth grade in an English-speaking school. He was acquiring Vietnamese when he was first exposed to English by his older siblings and members of his community. Like Isabella, his cultural community switches between Vietnamese and English. Kim has received English as a second language (ESL) services since kindergarten, yet he will likely continue to require ongoing language and academic support to bolster his below-grade-level English literacy and academic skills. Long-Term ELs are sometimes referred to as sequential or successive bilinguals (Hill & Miller, 2013).

Newcomer with Adequate Formal Schooling Jamal, now 12 years old and in the 6th grade, arrived from Pakistan 2 years ago with his parents, who are both college-educated speakers of Urdu. Before their move, Jamal regularly attended school in Pakistan. Although standardized assessments are sometimes still difficult, he is performing at or near grade level in reading and writing and is gaining oral English skills quickly.

Newcomer with Limited Formal Schooling Rima, 14 years old and in 9th grade, arrived in the United States last year from Syria after living in a refugee camp for 2 years. Her parents only attended a couple of years of school themselves and have only basic Arabic reading and writing skills. Rima's schooling was interrupted several times as they scrambled to flee from violent areas. Several of her family members were killed. She has limited L1 language and little to no L1 literacy skills. Research suggests that it may take 7 to 10 years for ELs like Rima with limited or no schooling to catch up to non-EL peers (Thomas & Collier, 2003).

In summary, factors such as learners' backgrounds, exposure to English, and history of formal schooling all add significantly to the variability among ELs. If you keep in mind what Annette learned—that vast differences in learner variability exists among ELs—you will be better able to plan for their needs.

HOW LANGUAGE AND CULTURE SHAPE LEARNING

Both language and culture shape learning. Therefore, we cannot discuss how language affects learner variability without considering how culture impacts learning. Language and culture are interwoven, interdependent characteristics that influence learning during every experience and in every learning environment. As students develop language to describe their experiences, it is their culture that provides them with cognitive tools for making sense of them and assigning meaning to them.

A description of culture that aligns well with the three neural networks states that culture is learned through socialization and consists of identifiable "...shared patterns of behaviors and interactions, cognitive constructs, and affective understandings" (Center for Advanced Research on Language Acquisition, University of Minnesota, 2009, p. 1). Cultural values and beliefs can determine how learners apply their affective networks in response to such aspects as gesturing, body proximity, gender roles, and personal autonomy (Hanley & Noblit, 2009; Zion & Kozleski, 2005). Consider these examples:

- When Dang's teacher asked students to indicate their progress with a thumbs-up motion, she was shocked because in her culture it is an obscene gesture.

- Although his teacher was trying to make him feel included, Feng was uncomfortable when his teacher sat close to him during reading circle.

- Chaka refused to participate in an oral class debate because her culture views assertiveness by females as unseemly.

- Growing up in a community that values collective harmony, Dawa was confused by the individual competitiveness he encountered in his new American classroom.

Cultural experiences also form the foundation for learners' recognition networks and provide unique perceptions, imagery, reasoning frameworks, and ways of defining their experiences. As depicted in figure 2.3, learners grow up and learn in varied environments resulting in very different cultural experiences that impact their language skills. For example, Northern Alaskans have more than 50 words for *snow* and Zulus use almost 40 words for the color *green* (Center for International Competence, 2017).

FIGURE 2.3: Snow vs. green: Differences in experiences affect perceptions.
© ELI BROPHY, PHILADELPHIA, PA

Culturally based problem-solving strategies can significantly shape learners' strategic networks. According to the National Center for Research on Cultural Diversity and Second Language Learning (1992), in contrast to some cultures that rely on inductive reasoning (i.e., going from general to specific), American culture tends to teach analytic, deductive thinking (i.e., going from specific to general).

Consequently, learners from varying cultures may construct problems or develop solutions in divergent ways. During an open-ended organizing task, students from one culture may organize elements based on functional and part-whole relationship, whereas those from another culture may group items based on categorical labels (Nisbett, Peng, Choi, & Norenzayan, 2001). This cognitive difference manifests itself among all learners and amplifies the learner variability that exists within a group of CLD students or ELs.

> *Cyclical in nature, the process of learning constantly shapes the learner's brain by creating neural pathways as the learner has various experiences.*

Cyclical in nature, the process of learning constantly shapes the learner's brain by creating neural pathways as the learner has various experiences. Because each learner has different experiences, even when doing the same tasks within the same learning environment, each learner develops different strengths, skills, interests, desires, and readiness levels that make up the individual's learner variability. This is particularly apparent among learners from different cultural and linguistic backgrounds.

Let's recap: Although each individual brain is distinct, learner variability is organized in a systematic, predictable way into three broad networks: Affective, Recognition, and Strategic. The UDL framework addresses the three learning networks through three UDL principles: Engagement, Representation, and Action and Expression. Keep in mind that language and culture have extraordinary influence on learning. Therefore, cultural and linguistic variability is a critical aspect to consider when planning for CLD students and ELs.

A WORD OF CAUTION

Cultures are dynamic, not static. So is learning. Cultural identities can change and do, sometimes quickly. Individuals develop personal identities that are aggregations of millions of experiences and inter-actions influenced by such aspects as gender, socioeconomic status, religion, physical attributes, birth order, age, and sexual preferences. Checklists based on stereotypic cultural assumptions can lead you to grouping decisions that deny learners the opportunity to be unique (Zion & Kozleski, 2005). Keep in mind that learners may identify as members of cultural groups but they also have a myriad of other group associations that affect their learning. In fact, CLD students and ELs have a multitude of experiences every day that shape their individual strengths, skills, interests, desires, and readiness level. As Annette discovered, learner variability is the one common denominator you can count on.

REFLECTION QUESTIONS

1. What barriers or difficulties did you experience when you studied a second or foreign language? How is your experience with learning a second language similar or different from the ELs in your classroom?

2. To what extent does learner variability exist in your teaching context? What range of variability do you see?

3. In what way might an English-only learning environment be enabling or disabling for ELs?

4. What other cultures, besides racial or ethnic cultures, might influence learner variability?

5. In what way do you feel bilingualism aids academic learning for ELs?

CHECK-IN: REFLECT ON LEARNER VARIABILITY

How do the three UDL principles (multiple means of Representation, multiple means of Action & Expression, multiple means of Engagement) address learner variability in CLD students and ELs? How does thinking about learner variability help educators design effective lessons for CLDs and ELs?

CHECK-IN: REFLECT ON LEARNER VARIABILITY

QUESTIONS ABOUT VARIABILITY ALIGNED WITH THE UDL FRAMEWORK	YOUR THOUGHTS AND IDEAS
How do learners, both EL and non-EL, differ in how they prefer to access information and concepts?	
How do learners, both EL and non-EL, differ in how they prefer to express what they have learned (e.g., orally, in writing, drawing, building, discussing, presenting)?	
How do learners, both EL and non-EL, differ in how they engage with concepts (e.g., what interests or motivates different learners, what bores learners)?	

3

Culturally Responsive Teaching and UDL

This chapter brings together suggested practices of Culturally Responsive Teaching (CRT) and UDL by presenting a crosswalk of UDL and seven principles of CRT proposed by Brown University, and offering suggestions specific to the principles of UDL.

Meet Lydia

Lydia, an eighth-grade social studies teacher, had the rare opportunity to attend two workshops in the past two months and both really got her thinking. One was about Culturally Responsive Teaching (CRT) and the other was about Universal Design for Learning (UDL). She knew she needed to learn more about CRT but was surprised by her takeaways. She went into the professional development workshop thinking she would learn certain strategies that she could embed in her lessons; she left understanding that she needs to continue having deeper conversations about her own sense of culture, and how her ingrained culture impacts her decisions and attitudes.

Lydia also realized that she needs to consciously lessen unintended bias and increase the exposure of students to all sorts of cultures to help them see how culture shapes their lives, too. It was a lot of new information to consider, but Lydia felt empowered, thinking about being able to have such a strong, positive influence on her culturally and linguistically diverse (CLD) and English learners (ELs).

The other workshop on UDL surprised her, too. Lydia was familiar with UDL's principles and Guidelines and had done some work around choosing teaching practices that align with the framework. What she hadn't recognized before was the central premise of UDL: to support the development of expert learners. Now it was making sense! Now she understood the intent of UDL and she agreed with it! The only question was how she could bring the information from the two workshops together. How was she going to make it all work in her classroom?

IT'S ALL IN THE LEARNING ENVIRONMENT

As Lydia discovered, the purpose of UDL is to support the development of expert learners. Discussed in chapter 1, expert learners are motivated and find purpose in their work. They understand how to set a goal and employ strategies to reach that goal. And, while they become skillful and knowledgeable about topics, they also become knowledgeable about their own learning and abilities. It is the role of expert teachers to create opportunities for students to learn and develop these skills.

REFLECTION How does UDL and its purpose translate into day-to-day practice? When you look at the UDL Guidelines, a word that stands out is *options*. Each Guideline begins with the words "Provide options for..." To what extent are you providing options now?

The language of the UDL Guidelines helps us understand a couple of things. First, we need to provide our students with different opportunities so they can build expert learner skills. Let's say they have only one opportunity or one way to complete a product. If that one opportunity fell on a day they were disconnected from learning, or the one way offered did not resonate with them as learners, then they missed out.

Second, options can be built into the environment so you're not re-creating them for each lesson or every student. For example, you can provide options around decoding—students can read silently on their own, read with a partner, listen to the book via an MP3 player and earbuds plugged into a splitter, or read the book on a screen and have the ability to click on words to view their definitions. Obviously, some of these options might not be available to all teachers—especially those options involving technology. However, such options as buddy readers, small groups, and independent reading are always available to any classroom. The point is, teachers can always create options so that all students have the opportunity to improve their decoding skills. However, it's also important to consider other dimensions of a UDL-inspired learning environment.

Some parts of our learning environment are fairly static (e.g., placement of bookshelves; placement of bulletin board; the spot where students hand in homework, projects, or other assessments) and some parts change with the lesson (e.g., when and how students use mini whiteboards, when and how students use laptops, when students read books from the classroom library, the ways students access print). Another key component of the learning environment is relationships: relationships between the teacher and the students, relationships between students, and relationships between students and other adults in that setting. Implementing UDL causes us to consider not just *where* we place furniture or workstations, *what* tools we're using, or *how* we interact with our students, but why, how, and when we're using spaces, resources, and strategies. Are we creating an accessible learning environment or an inaccessible one? And when we think about accessibility, are we expanding that concept to consider the design of culturally responsive environments?

UDL-CRT CROSSWALK

UDL and CRT are powerful frameworks that can lead to improved student outcomes, but because they are separate and distinct, it can be overwhelming to bring them together. And although UDL has a defined, systematic structure, CRT is described from a variety of angles in the literature. A constant theme emerges from the CRT literature: teachers and learners benefit from seeing ourselves as cultural beings who are part of a cultural palette, constantly investigating how we interact with and relate to other cultures. Barriers to our interactions include the following:

- The hidden curriculum—the beliefs, values, and norms woven into daily operations, teaching strategies, and rules that might only be apparent to the culture that created them

- Implicit bias—internalized, unconscious decision making based on stereotypic associations

- Stereotype threat—associating ability or lack of ability with a culture

- Microaggressions—intended or unintended comments seen as part of regular conversation that can degrade the recipient

Because these and other related issues are such an important part of designing the learning environment, they will be discussed in more detail in chapter 4.

To operationalize the pedagogy of CRT, Brown University (2017) compiled the work of 22 different authors and organizations to establish some of the most consistent characteristics of CRT:

- Positive perspectives on parents and families

- Communication of high expectations

- Learning within the context of culture

- Student-centered instruction

- Culturally mediated instruction

- Reshaping the curriculum

- Teacher as facilitator

This chapter shares the seven CRT principles in the order they are presented by Brown University's website and crosswalks them with the three principles of UDL. An overview of each CRT principle is provided prior to the individual table. Suggestions based on the UDL Guidelines and checkpoints within each principle are aligned with each CRT principle. Though these tables contain ideas, they are not intended to act as recipes. Instead, the reader is encouraged to take time and study the link between the CRT principle and the UDL principles. As DiAngelo and Sensoy (2010) point out, it is best when educators realize that there are no easy answers when practicing CRT. Expert educators are instead "willing to continue the practice of critical analysis" (p. 98).

> ▶ **Breaking News!**
>
> The Education Alliance at the Brown University website provides a single-sheet description of each of the seven characteristics of Culturally Responsive Teaching. Go to *http://ow.ly/ rwcp309W4Vv.*

POSITIVE PERSPECTIVE ON PARENTS AND FAMILIES

Parents and families should be engaged in conversations about the vital role they hold in their child's development. To remain culturally responsive, the conversation must include the parents' dreams and aspirations for their child. Educators must also discover alternatives beyond traditional parent participation models (Brown University, 2017).

Though these tables contain ideas, they are not intended to act as recipes. Instead, the reader is encouraged to take time and study the link between the CRT principle and the UDL principles.

There are two major assumptions that take place in a culturally responsive learning environment in relation to parents and families. First, we must presume that all parents and families are interested in their child's education. To believe otherwise would change how you interact with parents and families as well as their child. Second, though we don't typically think of parents and families as learners, they are. We all are. As we teach students, we need to learn about them and how they learn outside of school. We turn that information into classroom strategies to improve their outcomes (read more about this in chapter 4). At the same time, parents and families learn new information about your classroom, the school, and the educational system. Making that information accessible is equally as important. As seen in table 3.1, using the UDL framework in alignment with the principles and components of CRT can make the learning journey more accessible.

TABLE 3.1: UDL-CRT crosswalk: Positive perspective on parents and families

ENGAGEMENT	REPRESENTATION	ACTION AND EXPRESSION
Presume all parents and families are interested in their child's education. Ask parents and families to discover what information they'd like to see in newsletters/classroom announcements. Offer parents and families options to participate in different modes of communication (e.g., phone, email, school communication system). While suggesting ways parents can be involved in their child's education (e.g., reading to them, asking what they enjoyed learning that day, or participating in classroom activities), ask parents and families ways they would like to be involved in the school community.	Make all communications to parents accessible by avoiding jargon, using straightforward language, and providing the communication in text and digitally. Inform parents of free online text-to-speech tools (go to *http://udltechtoolkit. wikispaces.com/Free+ text+to+speech* for information) that will read aloud websites, newsletters, and in some cases, provide translation. Create a school year calendar with icons to represent major events (e.g., a star icon to signify statewide testing, a home icon to signify days when school is not in session, a smiley face icon to indicate parent–teacher conferences, and a plus sign to indicate when grade cards are distributed). Be sure to include a key.	Offer sessions to parents on how to use online text-to-speech tools. When meeting with parents, provide ample time (e.g., pause-and-reflect breaks) for their response and questions. Confirm with parents and families that multimedia tools used during face-to-face meetings enhance understanding rather than block communication. When using multimedia to present information to parents during face-to-face meetings, explain how the tool or technology is used in the classroom during instruction. Find out the dreams and aspirations parents and families have for their child. Bridge those desires with school. Share with them how the curriculum you are teaching will support those desired outcomes.

COMMUNICATING HIGH EXPECTATIONS

Studies show that students are significantly affected by the expectations set by teachers (Hattie, 2009); therefore, high expectations related to academic rigor must be set for all students and those expectations should be communicated by teachers, administrators, school counselors, and other school personnel. Learning goals should be consistently communicated using a variety of modalities (e.g., verbal, written, visual symbols). Educators must remember that how students respond to expectations as well as rigor will always be linked to norms associated with the student's culture (Brown University, 2017). Table 3.2 expands the use of UDL to the CRT principle of communicating high expectations.

Suggesting that we maintain high expectations probably doesn't feel revolutionary or a necessary conversation, but it is. We lower our expectations when we perceive the challenges our students face will be too great based on their overall lives (e.g., academic, home, social, and emotional). What's even more challenging is that lower expectations of CLD students are often so ingrained, they are tucked into our day-to-day perceptions (Gee, 1996; Mattia, Wagle, & Williams, 2010). This is why we need to purposefully examine what our expectations are and how we are designing an environment that upholds high expectations and maintains rigor.

To maintain rigor, we need to have an understanding of what we mean by *rigor*. Williamson and Blackburn (2010) state that rigor has nothing to do with additional homework, classwork, or even schoolwork that is extremely hard. Rather, rigor is an understanding that all students achieve at high levels only when high levels of work are "expected and inspected" (Early, Rogge, & Deci, 2014, p. 223). With that understanding, we begin to recognize that rigor is directly linked to the instructional and social-emotional opportunities we provide to our students.

TABLE 3.2: UDL-CRT crosswalk: Communicating high expectations

ENGAGEMENT	REPRESENTATION	ACTION AND EXPRESSION
Have students brainstorm coping skills and where they learned those skills. Use suggestions to create a menu of coping options. Post and discuss the goal for each lesson. Establish an environment where students safely explore and communicate their cultural norms with their classmates. Help students develop healthy self-concept through mastery-oriented feedback.	Unearth the hidden curriculum of the classroom and school—the social, emotional, and behavioral expectations assumed to be known and practiced—and supply that background knowledge to all students. Communicate high expectations consistently and via different modes and media (e.g., verbal, written, music, poetry, stories). Break down expectations into smaller components or achievable steps.	Provide students with a way to chart or watch their growth toward the set expectations. Assess progress as well as outcomes. Have students suggest ways they can demonstrate knowledge/skills and communicate their own meaning. Examine classroom behavioral expectations alongside the norms of your students' cultural experiences.

Robyn Jackson, a former educator and administrator, describes four outcomes students demonstrate in a rigorous classroom (Allen, 2012). UDL helps us design for these outcomes via Guideline-related methods, materials, and assessment strategies. Table 3.3 aligns selected UDL Guidelines with rigorous outcomes.

TABLE 3.3: UDL and outcomes of the rigorous classroom

SELECTED UDL GUIDELINES	OUTCOMES OF RIGOROUS CLASSROOM
Provide options for: • Recruiting interest • Comprehension • Perception • Physical action	"Students know how to create their own meaning out of what they learn" (p. 3).
Provide options for: • Comprehension • Perception • Expression and communication • Physical action	"They organize information so they create mental models" (p. 3).
Provide options for: • Self-regulation • Sustaining effort and persistence • Comprehension • Language, mathematical expressions, and symbols • Expression and communication	"They integrate individual skills into whole sets of processes" (p. 3).
Provide options for: • Sustaining effort and persistence • Comprehension • Language, mathematical expressions, and symbols • Executive functions • Expression and communication	"They apply what they've learned to new or novel situations" (p. 3).

LEARNING WITHIN THE CONTEXT OF CULTURE

This principle points to the potential disconnect when the context of the home and the context of school do not closely correspond. A disconnect could stem from diverse languages spoken, how learning takes place, or how relationships are built and could manifest as different behaviors, communication, types of expectations, and even the size of one's personal space (Brown University, 2017). Table 3.4 illustrates contrasts between individualism and collectivism, though Hammond (2015) clarifies that people living in collectivist cultures still experience the culture in their own way.

TABLE 3.4: Features of the individualist and collective cultures

INDIVIDUALISM	COLLECTIVISM
Focused on independence and individual achievement	Focused on interdependence and group success
Emphasizes self-reliance and the belief that you are supposed to take care of yourself to get ahead	Emphasizes reliance on the collective wisdom or resources of the group and the belief that group members take care of each other to get ahead
Learning happens through individual study and reading	Learning happens through group interaction and dialogue
Individual contribution and status are important	Group dynamics and harmony are important
Competitive	Collaborative
Technical/analytical	Relational

The important takeaways from the individualism–collectivism continuum is that (1) cultural determinations have a deep impact on how our students experience learning in their communities, and (2) how they learn in their communities directly impacts how they learn in the classroom (Gay, 2010; Hammond, 2015). By providing a range of learning experiences that span the individualism–collectivism continuum, an educator can provide culturally relevant learning opportunities for all students.

As described in chapter 2, all learning and behavior is the result of our individual interaction with context (Rose, Rouhani, & Fischer, 2013), and that interaction impacts how we, as individuals, express our culture. Each of us accrues cultural or social capital as we learn and grow (Hanley & Noblit, 2009; Waitoller & Thorius, 2016). Cultural capital does not refer to financial wealth but instead to the assets we can use to influence others and to be successful within our society. It includes specialized knowledge, state of mind, how we express and conduct ourselves with others, and personal belongings associated with our individual cultural identities. Learning within the context of the dominant culture with continuing experiences in their home environments, CLD students and ELs gain cultural capital assets in more than one culture. Teachers can help students effectively use these assets in the learning environment. Table 3.5 provides a crosswalk between the UDL framework and examples of CRT strategies that address learning within the context of culture.

TABLE 3.5: UDL-CRT crosswalk: Learning within the context of culture

ENGAGEMENT	REPRESENTATION	ACTION AND EXPRESSION
Guide students to explore a variety of coping skills, some of which might be outside of their cultural norms but might resonate with them. Because students will vary in their preference for working independently or collaboratively, provide options for both. In situations where no option is provided, offer scaffolds and clear expectations to build student effort and persistence. Options for choice and autonomy that also have the students think about their choices (e.g., why are they choosing this option versus another) help them build knowledge about themselves as individual learners within the context of school and the context of their culture. Acknowledge to the students that how they learn in the school setting might be different than their home setting. Be willing to bring other learning structures into your classroom environment.	Guide students to examine how they learn in their home/community and how that is or is not reflected in their school-based learning. Guide students' understanding that when the context of home and the context of school is very different, that is not a bad thing. Through modeling, help them discover and bridge the differences. When the home language is different than the classroom language, provide scaffolds for language and symbols. When available, provide low- and high-tech options for alternatives to auditory and visual information (e.g., picture cards that align with written vocabulary, recorded books).	Guide students to understand how their culture impacts their preferences for expression. Next, empower students to explore a variety of digital and nondigital tools as a way to express their knowledge. Ensure students have the opportunity to work both collaboratively and independently throughout projects and have them reflect on their preferences and investigate how those preferences relate to their culture. How students are reminded to complete a task when at home or in their community could differ from methods used in the classroom. Offer a variety of prompts, coaching, and mentoring so students can discover strategies that align with their needs.

STUDENT-CENTERED INSTRUCTION

Student-centered instruction is an approach that emphasizes teachers as facilitators of active learning by students rather than mere transmitters of knowledge. It shifts attention in the classroom away from what teachers do at the front of the class to what students accomplish in their seats or in cooperative groups or in project-based learning. Teachers become a "guide on the side" rather than a "sage on the stage" (King, 1993). Student-centered learned emphasizes the interaction between teacher and students and among students themselves, rather than a one-way lecture format with teachers simply addressing students. The core question related to student-centered instruction is "How will I be sure my students will meet the outcomes they're supposed to meet if I'm not directly guiding their learning?" Student-centered lesson design incorporates collaboration—as well as cooperative and community-oriented options—that are culturally relevant to students.

Several elements are pivotal to ensure students meet desired outcomes in a culturally responsive environment. First, students need to feel a connection to what they're learning. As discussed previously, when you adapt the curriculum to students' interests, they become personally involved. When students become personally involved, they take more ownership of their learning. When student ownership exists, they are more likely to take a stronger lead in their own learning (Checkley, 1995).

Next, the lesson needs to be constructed to provide students with scaffolds that help them take the lead. For example, a teacher provides the students in his social studies classes with rubrics, checklists, and e-tools, such as online translations and embedded supports that target anticipated learning needs (Meyer, Rose, & Gordon, 2014; Nelson, 2014; Rose & Meyer, 2002). Although it is natural to choose the scaffolds based on perceived and known student needs, scaffold selection is also based on the goal of the lesson. By adding scaffolds based on the learning goal, you offer flexibility without lowering expectations (Ralabate, 2016).

A third element comes at the beginning of the lesson. Students must understand the objective of the lesson and activity. They need to know the goal. They need to know what they are to learn and understand that they will be formatively assessed on their knowledge. Directly related to rigor and high expectations, formative assessment allows students to articulate their current knowledge or skill proficiency without being graded and allows teachers to shift the current and future instruction to narrow any gaps in understanding (Greenstein, 2010).

Just these three elements of establishing student-centered instruction can feel overwhelming, but as Nelson (2014) phrases it, start small. Begin with brief activities that allow students to take more ownership in their learning, making clear to them that they are doing so, and making it clear that they will take more and more ownership over time. By starting small, you and your students get used to this new way of learning and teaching.

As mentioned above, students will vary in their ability to maintain levels of engagement and resourcefulness, and in their ability to set goals and strategize how they will move through projects and assignments, both on their own and collaboratively. Examples in table 3.6 exemplify how the UDL framework can support the design of an environment that guides students toward these outcomes.

TABLE 3.6: UDL-CRT crosswalk: Student-centered instruction

ENGAGEMENT	REPRESENTATION	ACTION AND EXPRESSION
Provide a variety of ways students can self-assess and reflect on the quality of their work and their effort (e.g., journaling, teacher-student check-ins, rubrics, and/or graphic organizers). Require students to articulate a learning goal for their research or project and set daily outcomes. These become their touchstone when the process feels unwieldy. Some students require support in how to collaborate; however, how students collaborate will tie directly to their culture. Though it is helpful for students to understand roles and responsibilities within collaborative learning, be attentive to cultural dynamics (e.g., individualistic versus collective learning, body language and gestures) and allow for a mix of the two.	Provide guiding protocols or procedures for students to follow during student-directed learning. Conduct consistent check-ins with students to ensure they see how their day-to-day work is connected to the big picture, to their larger research question or assignment. Guide students toward resource and research tool options. Provide guidance on how to use resources and research tools when necessary. When available, provide opportunities for students to explore digital tools that scaffold learning. At a minimum, have students learn how to find quality definitions/ translations and how to discover reliable resources for factual information.	Provide scaffolds (e.g., rubrics, checklists, pair check-ins, setting daily or weekly learning targets) to support executive functioning, which is necessary in student-centered instruction. Encourage students to explore a variety of media to share their research and work (e.g., PowerPoint, Prezi, or PowToons). Such tools provide a platform for students to express personal preference and culturally relevant images. Guide student understanding of the standards and learning goals so they can choose appropriate, culturally relevant topics and subjects.

CULTURALLY MEDIATED INSTRUCTION

When instruction is culturally mediated, multicultural viewpoints are welcomed and encouraged. Students are provided with a variety of ways to know, understand, and represent the information they are learning. In addition, the relationships between students and teachers are in harmony with students' cultures (Brown University, 2017).

The use of multicultural viewpoints has been discussed throughout this chapter. We know that by encouraging students to contribute artifacts and their own stories to the classroom environment, we take an initial step toward establishing multicultural viewpoints. Within the culturally mediated instruction principle, one dynamic we have not yet considered is the relationship between students and teachers. Psychology and education research is filled with studies promoting the development of positive and strong relationships between students and teachers. Rimm-Kaufman & Sandilos (n.d.) pull from over eighty-four references and offer straightforward, school-specific examples focusing on issues such as what positive teacher-student relationships look like in the classroom to how to cultivate those relationships. Some examples include prompts such as, "How to cultivate positive relationships in your classroom." The following scenario provides a response to this question:

> Angel, whose L1 is Spanish, asks his teacher about English vocabulary associated with the current lesson. After his teacher, Marie, answers his question, she asks him what the vocabulary word is in Spanish and how he'd use it in a sentence. By responding in this way, Marie demonstrates not only that she cares about Angel as a student but that she also is aware of his unique strengths (i.e., fluency in another language).

The principle of culturally mediated instruction goes further and asks teachers to discover how students learn in their communities, at home, or a different school setting (also see the section "Funds of Knowledge" in chapter 4). Because there's no way to memorize all the nuances related to each culture, one suggestion is to turn to others who share the same culture as the student. Have conversations with teaching peers, community leaders, and parents (Brown University, 2017; Hollins, 1996; Nieto, 1996). In addition, you can look to work conducted by New York University's Metropolitan Center for Urban Education, which focused on Culturally Responsive Classroom Management (CRCM) in their whitepaper (2008). They identified five elements of CRCM. The last one, commitment to building caring classroom communities, directly addresses this CRT principle.

The CRCM whitepaper describes how different teachers chose specific actions to establish connections. One teacher wanted his students to know their perspective mattered, so at the end of his math class each day, they wrote in their journals and addressed the following prompt: "How did I do as a teacher today?" (Metropolitan Center for Urban Education, 2008, p. 5). A researcher found that urban educators who had established trusting relationships with their students had done so through out-of-class conversations where they got to know the students personally. The teachers initiated these conversations. The researcher also found that these teachers engaged the students in social games and established school-to-home relationships (Brown, 2003).

Greeting students at the door, expressing interest and admiration for multilingual speakers, and commenting positively on the number of languages spoken and represented in the classroom all lead to positive outcomes (Weinstein, Tomlinson-Clarke, & Curran, 2004). And Marzano, Marzano, and Pickering (2003) stated that showing interest in students as individuals has a positive impact. Examples such as being aware of important events in their lives like sports events, theater, or other extracurricular activities; greeting the students when outside the classroom; and specifically making time to talk to them each day in the lunchroom were all suggestions. As shown in table 3.7, the UDL framework supports all these ideas.

TABLE 3.7: UDL-CRT crosswalk: Culturally mediated instruction

ENGAGEMENT	REPRESENTATION	ACTION AND EXPRESSION
There is an expectation that culturally mediated and multicultural viewpoints will be expressed to enhance the learning environment. Students are encouraged to self-assess and reflect on how their own cultural experiences impact their learning. The learning environment becomes a safe environment for discussions about the impact of culture on learning and living. Provide opportunities to establish a community within the classroom that upholds and celebrates the uniqueness of each student.	Provide students with instruction on concept mapping, and encourage journaling and other strategies to guide students' ability to process complex conversations about culture. Help students build vocabulary to enhance deeper conversations about cultural diversity. Provide students with ample media opportunities to explore culture, both theirs and other cultures. Provide scaffolds to support students' processing and consideration of issues that impact them.	Help students identify goals related to personal growth in understanding their own culture and cultures around them. Help students identify how to monitor their own growth in cultural responsiveness. Provide opportunities for students to explore media and other tools as ways to express their cultural interpretations and identities. Provide students with opportunities to share their perspectives on academic and social issues.

RESHAPING THE CURRICULUM

A culturally responsive curriculum is integrated, interdisciplinary, meaningful, and student-centered. Course issues and topics relate to students' backgrounds and challenge higher-order thinking (Brown University, 2017).

An interdisciplinary curriculum is integral to the overall concept of an integrated curriculum (Drake & Burns, 2004). It focuses on theme, concepts, and interdisciplinary skills such as literacy skills, thinking, numeracy, and research skills (Drake & Burns, 2004). The key is that students are learning skills and concepts beyond a specific lesson.

In an interdisciplinary curriculum, educators *integrate* issues and topics related to the students' background rather than *adapt* the curriculum to include issues and topics. Who the students are and their experiences become the drivers for the curriculum and standards. Consequently, this type of curriculum provides more flexibility for Culturally Responsive Design. And because it focuses on building interdisciplinary skills, it helps build higher-order thinking skills.

Higher-order thinking skills involve learners taking their own thinking beyond the information that was given to them. They engage in learning experiences like argumentation, critiquing, organizing, project-based learning, discovery learning, and reasoning (Torff, 2003). These skills are developed through learner-centered teaching, which facilitates the construction of knowledge. The opposite type of teaching is didactic, teacher-led instruction, which is more curriculum-focused, where students are receptacles of information and have limited learner participation and reflection (Johnes, 2006).

As shown in table 3.8, the UDL framework helps us design instruction to develop interdisciplinary skills as well as higher-order thinking skills, while focusing on culturally responsive issues and topics.

TABLE 3.8: UDL-CRT crosswalk: Reshaping the curriculum

ENGAGEMENT	REPRESENTATION	ACTION AND EXPRESSION
Students' cultural lives should be reflected in the curriculum, topics, and materials. Teachers can foster community and collaboration through the use of both group work and independent work. Students learn to value both and respect when their peers choose one or the other.	Support students' ability to recognize inherent knowledge they have based on cultural experiences and how their background knowledge links to learning. Support the transfer and generalization of knowledge students have gained based on culturally based experiences to what they are learning in the classroom.	Provide students with the opportunity to explore multiple strategies to solve problems/discover answers to their questions. This includes exploring alternative viewpoints or beliefs on a topic. Support students to take ownership of what they are learning. This happens when they experience success in applying the knowledge they have gained.

TEACHER AS FACILITATOR

The learning environment refers to the permanent and semipermanent structures within the space used for teaching—everything from interactive bulletin boards to desk arrangement. A learning environment can be the classroom, gymnasium, cafeteria, theater, hallways, counselor's office, playground, outdoor garden, or anywhere instruction is offered. Ultimately, UDL has us consider whether the semipermanent and permanent structures are accessible to all students and provide flexible learning opportunities.

For example, if students are utilizing the bulletin board to pick up assignments, are they choosing from two or more options or is it simply a point of distribution for a single assignment? When considering the desks, are they always configured the same way, or are they reconfigured based on the goal of the lesson and associated grouping structures? And if they are reconfigured, is it often enough that students are accustomed to the pattern shift and the expectations related to this more social organization? When the learning environment is operated with accessibility and flexibility in mind, students' social, cultural, and linguistic needs can be more easily met. Table 3.9 suggests some options.

TABLE 3.9: UDL-CRT crosswalk: Teacher as facilitator

ENGAGEMENT	REPRESENTATION	ACTION AND EXPRESSION
Relevancy, value, and authenticity will come from students sharing information and artifacts that reflect their culture. Relevance, value, and authenticity will come from students sharing their experiences in a variety of formats. Students practice the skills of choice and autonomy by choosing books approved by the teacher but that suit the students' individual interests.	Teach vocabulary through concrete objects and demonstration. Relate math problems and vocabulary to background knowledge. Apply problems to daily life situations. Use manipulatives to make problems concrete. Establish explicit interdisciplinary connections for students.	Students are provided with multiple opportunities and ways to share experiences that reflect their culture. Students build planning and strategy development skills by leading discussion groups. Suggest strategies for goal-setting and monitor students on their growth in this skill set.

Lydia's Next Steps

When Lydia left the two workshops on UDL and CRT, she wondered how she was going to make it all work together in her classroom. She thought about where she was in relationship to the seven principles and chose to begin with positive perspectives on parent and families. Her principal had begun the year by asking teachers to establish better relationships with families and to document their efforts. Up to this point, that had felt like "one more thing," but now Lydia realized it was part of establishing a culturally responsive environment and that she could use what she learned about UDL to help her design her outreach.

First, she connected with other teachers in the building with whom she shared her students to see how they were reaching out to parents who weren't native English speakers. One teacher had found success suggesting Google Translate. It wasn't perfect but it was a good starting point. The parents were very appreciative of the suggestion and reported having a much better idea of what was going on in the classroom than they did before.

The next thing Lydia did was work with her grade-level team to add symbols to their calendar. Once they came up with a system, they shared it with the staff, who agreed to use the same symbols; the whole school calendar was updated. These two steps spread out over time. Lydia knew she wasn't done creating a more culturally responsive environment, but she knew she was on her way and UDL had helped.

In summary, this chapter clarified how the act of designing culturally responsive lessons and learning environments is a thoughtful process. Brown University's seven principles provide a structure to investigate how UDL intersects with CRT. They are: (1) positive perspectives on parents and families, (2) communication of high expectations,

(3) learning within the context of culture, (4) student-centered instruction, (5) culturally mediated instruction, (6) reshaping the curriculum, and (7) teacher as facilitator. This chapter provided a breakdown of each principle and offered suggestions on how CRT aligns with UDL.

REFLECTION QUESTIONS

1. In what additional ways do you see the seven CRT principles and UDL overlap?

2. Which CRT principle might you focus on first and why?

3. How does higher-order thinking link with communicating high expectations and reshaping the curriculum?

4. How can you learn about your students' backgrounds, both ancestral and current?

5. How does CRT expand learning opportunities for all students?

CHECK-IN: QUESTIONS TO ASK ABOUT CRT AND YOUR TEACHING

1. I used to think CRT was: _____.

2. Now I know CRT is: _____.

3. I used to think I had to do _____ to create a culturally responsive lesson/environment.

4. Now I know I can _____ to create a culturally responsive lesson/environment.

The Culturally Responsive Learning Environment

4

This chapter explores the creation of culturally responsive learning environments for CLD students and ELs by looking at hidden barriers and the positive action staff can take to alleviate those barriers.

Meet Henderson

Henderson is in his fifth year of teaching in the same elementary school. His school is in a community with a multinational company, and families of the employees move to the United States for one to three years. It's common for new students from other countries to join his class well into the school year. In fact, nine languages were spoken in his classroom at one time last year. Not only have newcomers arrived from China, Korea, Mexico, the Philippines, and Germany, his American-born students are ethnically and linguistically diverse as well. At the beginning of the year, and when new students arrive, Henderson asks them to write paragraphs, cut out likenesses, or draw pictures representing themselves, their likes, and their hobbies, demonstrating this teacher's understanding of the importance of letting students celebrate their own culture and see themselves in his classroom.

But now, three months into the year, he begins to think he's missing something. He's always focused on what he'll have the students do. Now he wonders, "What about my own background, beliefs, and experiences? How do they fit into Culturally Responsive Teaching?"

THE LEARNING ENVIRONMENT

What is the learning environment? Introduced in chapter 3, the learning environment has three parts:

- The space in which learning takes place

- The why, how, and when we're using spaces, resources, and strategies

- Relationships

A rich learning environment encompasses the academic and social emotional needs experienced by every learner.

UDL helps us design a learning environment that is useful, empowering, and instructive to all students. It builds on each student's strengths—strengths that are grounded in each student's culture. Alternatively, if the learning environment is restrictive and does not allow interplay with each student's culture, their strengths can become deficits. For example, when a student does not see aspects of herself or her community represented within the design of the environment, she is in danger of an uncomfortable, unfamiliar, and alienating experience (Dimitriadis & Kamberelis, 2006). Some educators interpret this to mean they have to know and acknowledge every culture in their room.

Fortunately, Hammond (in Ferlazzo, 2015) shares that CRT is not about replicating a culture; it's more about mimicking the nuances of cultures. And while we learn about the students' cultures and how learning takes place, we use the UDL framework to look closely at our teaching strategies to ensure accessibility for all students. Fazillah's experience offers an example.

Fazillah knew that collaborative activities helped engage her students to connect more deeply with the topic (the UDL Guideline of sustaining effort and persistence), but she noticed that some of her students were not participating. She knew they were familiar with the content, but they just wouldn't speak up. After talking with her colleague Jiyeon, she learned that some of the students who were Asian American might benefit from protocols or clear directions defining when they should talk and when they should listen. Fazillah learned about "authoring," a cultural trait described by Tateishi (2014). Of course, she wasn't going to overgeneralize and believe it applied to every student of Asian descent student in her class. However, understanding that certain behaviors are traditionally valued in some cultures helped her to anticipate learner variability that might exist in her classroom.

Culturally, it was important to these students not to say too much because restraint is traditionally valued. They also needed to understand when they could or were supposed to talk. As she reflected further, Fazillah realized she could make the objectives of collaboration clearer for all students. In this way, she not only applied the UDL Guideline of sustaining effort and persistence, she also addressed the UDL Guideline of recruiting interest by minimizing threats associated with collaborative work and it was driven by the variable needs of her students.

Because Fazillah is open to exploring all aspects of who her learners are, she more effectively uses the UDL framework to design her lessons and move her students toward becoming expert learners.

Expert Learners

In chapter 1, you learned that UDL is a framework that guides students toward becoming expert learners. They participate in learning in a way that helps them gain skills that identify how to connect to their experiences and persevere through challenges. Students practice how to identify and glean knowledge from quality resources. They understand how to identify what they want to learn or experience and the steps necessary to lead them to that experience. Beyond content knowledge, these are the skills all learners need to succeed in any postsecondary setting.

Effective teachers are also expert learners. They continue to grow and learn. They look for ways to analyze their teaching, they model and mentor what it means to be a learner to their students, and they share their journey with others (Meyer, Rose, & Gordon, 2014). Some schools have professional learning communities or other collaborative structures where teachers have the opportunity to reflect and share. When these structures aren't in place, it is even more crucial that teachers identify how to connect and reflect with other professionals. Fundamentally, the act of becoming an expert learner mirrors the deep reflection that supports the development of culturally responsive learning environments.

Fundamentally, the act of becoming an expert learner mirrors the deep reflection that supports the development of culturally responsive learning environments.

This book has an intentional focus on English learners and the cultural diversity they bring to the classroom. That said, we recognize that the topic of Culturally Responsive Teaching brings to mind the diversity of students based on both culture and race. Therefore, this chapter will move slightly beyond the bounds of English learners to provide the reader with a broader understanding related to CRT. Finally, this chapter is written in alignment with Gay's (2013) stance that CRT is "more about finding solutions to achievement disparities in schools than simply casting dispersions on student and teachers" (pp. 54–55). A first step toward finding solutions to use in the classroom is to consider funds of knowledge.

Funds of Knowledge

How we see, think about, and react to the world is based on our background knowledge. Our background knowledge is grounded in our experiences, and as discussed earlier, many of our life experiences are grounded in, guided by, and directly associated with our culture. How we experience the world in our early years is directly influenced by our inner circle of family, friends, and community (Bronfenbrenner, 1981). As we grow older and begin to make our own choices about with whom we spend time, where we experience life, and how we experience life, we add to our background knowledge, which adds complexity to our relationship with our culture. Ultimately, though, our cultural background determines how we view and function within the world. Life experiences and relationships shape how we learn and express learning, which directly relates to a concept called *funds of knowledge*.

> ## ▶ Extending Your Knowledge
>
> While this chapter continues with a discussion about funds of knowledge and hidden barriers and then suggests points of reflection for educators to articulate the importance of CRT, we strongly suggest readers turn to leaders in the field, such as Wayne Au (2014), Geneva Gay (2010), Zarreta Hammond (2015), Elizabeth Kozleski (2008), Gloria Ladson-Billings (2001; 2009), and Beverly Daniel Tatum (1997) to enrich your knowledge.

The concept came from anthropology (Wolf, 1966), but it was researchers from the University of Arizona who connected funds of knowledge to education and established its meaning in schools (González, Moll, & Amanti, 2005). The original work focused on the cultural systems (e.g., home and social systems) of Mexican–U.S. children and how systems could positively influence instruction

(Vélez-Ibáñez & Greenberg, 1992), but funds of knowledge are now recognized as an important piece of educating students of all cultures (Subero, Vila, & Esteban-Guitart, 2015).

The three major objectives of funds of knowledge are: (1) improving academic outcomes of traditionally underserved students, (2) improving ties between families and schools, and (3) using funds of knowledge to modify teaching practices (González et al., 2005; Subero et al., 2015). Table 4.1 offers examples from research of ways teachers collected and utilized students' funds of knowledge (Hogg, 2011).

TABLE 4.1: Examples of how students' funds of knowledge align with UDL

AUTHOR	RESEARCH EXAMPLE	UDL ALIGNMENT
Moll, Amanti, Neff, & González, 1992	An elementary teacher saw a student selling Mexican candy, inspiring her to collaborate with students to design cross-curricular unit on candy.	Engagement • Recruiting interest Representation • Comprehension
Lee, 2001	A high school teacher used African American students' knowledge of signifying, a type of language play, in their study of literary works.	Engagement • Recruiting interest • Self-regulation Representation • Language, mathematical expressions, and symbols • Comprehension Action and expression • Expression and communication

AUTHOR	RESEARCH EXAMPLE	UDL ALIGNMENT
Olmedo, 1997	A teacher training guided the development of oral history tasks for social studies and history students. The activities ultimately helped students connect their lives and validate their views and perspectives, and supported them to become emerging historians.	Engagement • Recruiting interest • Sustaining effort and persistence Representation • Perception • Language, mathematical expressions, and symbols • Comprehension Action and expression • Expression and communication
Moll et al., 1992	Over a semester, a teacher brought together parents and community members who contributed to the development of lessons through information sharing. This collaboration developed a social network to identify students' funds of knowledge.	Engagement • Recruiting interest • Sustaining effort and persistence Representation • Language, mathematical expressions, and symbols • Comprehension

By definition, funds of knowledge are "practices that recognize, appreciate and make use of family and community knowledge pertaining to the less empowered students within the school" (Subero et al., 2015, p. 45). Referring further to Luis Moll, Cathy Amanti, Deborah Neff, and Norma González (2001), the researchers who developed the definition of funds of knowledge, Janet Keir Lopez points out that "When teachers shed their role of teacher and expert and, instead, take on a new role as learner, they can come to know their students and the families of their students in new and distinct ways. With this new knowledge, they can begin to see that the households of their students contain rich cultural and cognitive resources and that these resources can and should be used in their classroom in order to provide culturally responsive and meaningful lessons that tap students' prior knowledge" (Lopez, n.d.). Because families and communities are such a crucial piece to gathering funds of knowledge, we recommend looking more deeply into ways of effectively connecting with these home partners. Many national organizations, state departments of education, higher education centers, and a significant number of publications offer suggestions, strategies, and solutions to building effective and deep partnerships within any community. A brief list of those links and references appears in table 4.2.

TABLE 4.2: Suggestions for improving family and community partnerships

ORGANIZATIONS	SPECIFIC LINKS
National Education Association (NEA)	Parent, Family, Community Involvement in Education from the NEA: www.nea.org/assets/docs/PB11_ParentInvolvement08.pdf
Center for Parent Information and Resources	Parent involvement resources: www.parentcenterhub.org/topics/parentinvolvement/
Project Appleseed	www.projectappleseed.org
PACER Center	Culturally responsible parent involvement: www.pacer.org/mpc/pdf/CulturallyResponsivePI.pdf

ORGANIZATIONS	SPECIFIC LINKS
Schoolwide Integrated Framework for Transformation (SWIFT Center)	Trusting family partnerships: *http://guide.swiftschools.org/family-community-engagement/trusting-family-partnerships* Trusting community partnerships: *http://guide.swiftschools.org/family-community-engagement/trusting-community-partnerships*
Mexican American Legal Defense and Education Fund & the NEA	Minority parent and community engagement: *https://www.maldef.org/assets/pdf/mco_maldef%20report_final.pdf*
Ohio Department of Education	Sample best practices for parent involvement in schools from the Ohio Department of Education: *http://bit.ly/1PVs9Tl*

▶ **Breaking News!**

To learn more about funds of knowledge and to learn ways to access that information about your students, go to *www.learnnc.org/lp/pages/939*.

Funds of knowledge point to the great variation in students' knowledge bases, showing how they are expansive and not singular to one culture. Any one student or classroom will present a unique combination of intercultural cross-overs coming together as a hybrid of knowledge bases. Indeed, our youth culture uses our communicative and connected world to expand multiple cultural systems (González et al., 2005).

Our students have greater interconnectivity via the digital world. Digital tools provide the opportunity for exposure to more cultures in the classroom and on their own time. Their consumption of digital media has the potential to introduce them to traditions, experiences, and the daily life of others whom they would otherwise never meet. Relationships can be easily built with peers across the world, ignoring the once physical boundaries of the neighborhood. And when students are no longer encapsulated into a specific culture, the breadth of variability increases. Because we all have opportunities for digital communication, this is also true of adults. We, too, have funds of knowledge, and it is important for us to reflect on how our own varied backgrounds of knowledge affect our thinking and teaching. Because they are situated in our background knowledge and experiences, our funds of knowledge directly impact the design of our environments and lessons. That, in turn, directly affects our students. The process is cyclical (see figure 4.1). And, as we reflect on interactions with our students, our funds of knowledge are enhanced.

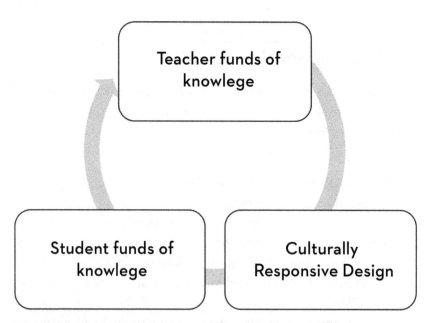

FIGURE 4.1: Cyclical nature of funds of knowledge and Culturally Responsive Design

The National Center for Education Statistics (2016) shares striking information: 45 percent of public school students are students of color, whereas over 80 percent of teachers are non-Latino white. In fact, non-Latino students earned more than 80 percent of the bachelor's degrees awarded in 2009–10 (Durey, 2010). Why does that matter? Because the background knowledge and experiences of most teachers do not align with the students they are teaching. Moreover, Hedges's research (2012) found that we prioritize our informal knowledge—the knowledge we gain through our own experiences, which includes broad or narrow exposure to cultures outside our own—over researched methods backed by theory and practice. Our own funds of knowledge can become a barrier to the success of our students whose cultures differ from ours. Moreover, Hedges (2012) proposed that we prioritize our informal knowledge over researched methods. Our use of own funds of knowledge becomes a barrier to our students' success.

This gap between the teachers' funds of knowledge and their students is yet another clear reason why multicultural education that includes the experiences, struggles, and celebrations of cultures needs to be infused throughout the entire curriculum and why we need multicultural education to help us create a rigorous curriculum for all learners (Au, 2014). How do we use this information reflectively and develop responsive lessons and learning environments? One way is to understand the potential barriers we might place in our students' paths.

Hidden Barriers

As described earlier, one of UDL's founding principles guides us to remove barriers to our students' learning. At its outset, the researchers at CAST who developed UDL focused on the creation of tools that students with disabilities could use in the general education environment. At the time, the researchers focused on interventions that helped "fix" learners' ability to learn. But as they grew in their understanding of the three networks and the underlying brain research, CAST researchers realized that it wasn't the learners who needed fixing; it was the learning environment, including curriculum, that needed to shift in order to support the inevitable variability that is always present in any classroom (Meyer, Rose, & Gordon, 2014). As the UDL framework and its guidelines began to be applied and implemented, inclusive practices, strategies, and tools for all students were designed in ways that asked educators to shift their thinking and anticipate possible barriers to learner understanding, expression of knowledge, and later engagement in learning. All this planning is in part guided by the educator's background knowledge and funds of knowledge, but what if some of our intentions are affected in a relatively unconscious way?

Researchers help us understand that unconscious barriers impact instruction (Langhout & Mitchell, 2008), but because these barriers are linked to culture, both educators and students experience them. Barriers need to be considered from both points of view. The following section provides a brief overview of the hidden curriculum, implicit bias, stereotype threat, and micro-aggressions. The section ends with purposeful conversations about race as a way educators can be attentive to hidden barriers. Each overview ends with how UDL can help mitigate the impact of that barrier or enhance the conversation. Thinking about hidden barriers to learning challenges us to think about ourselves as teachers and citizens within a multicultural society.

The Hidden Curriculum

Every individual brings to the learning environment a set of beliefs, norms, and values that were shaped by his or her culture. But individuals also *encounter* a set of beliefs, norms, and values that may be inherent to the learning environment but not clearly articulated. These latter reflect the viewpoints and experience of whoever designed the learning environment, and they constitute the "hidden curriculum" (Giroux & Penna, 1979; Wren, 1999). For example, at the entrance to a hypothetical school named Traditional High School their mascot is designed into the floor tiles. It is a ritual that no one steps on the mascot. When visitors, new students, and new-to-the-building substitutes step on the mascot, they are reprimanded by students, teachers, and administrators for disrespecting the school. Though stepping over or around the mascot brings pride to the community of Traditional High School, the action is a hidden value and is part of that school's hidden curriculum. The hidden curriculum is present for teachers, too.

Remember your first year of teaching? You had to learn if there were specific places people sat in the teachers' lunchroom or if teachers even ate in the lunchroom. You had to learn where groups sat during professional development, what group you belonged to, and whether it was the norm to be early or late. And over the course of the year, you learned how the school as a whole responded to certain student behaviors. No one taught you these things, but when or if you behaved outside of those established beliefs, norms, or values, you might have felt uncomfortable or out-of-step with your colleagues. Adults have a greater capacity to discover, align with, or negotiate around the hidden curriculum, but students don't arrive at school with that capacity.

Research dating back to 1968 (Jackson) documents the challenges students have following and internalizing the hidden curriculum, and the issue remains the same today. Students can become unsure how to act or react to academic or social situations. They might not internalize or follow classroom rules and daily routines, which can work against their personal and intellectual development and lead to discipline problems (Hale, 1994; Langhout & Mitchell, 2008; Persell, 1977; Rios, 1996).

Symbolic aspects of schools are a significant part of the hidden curriculum. Table 4.3 lists aspects, where they can be found, what they are, and the associated hidden curriculum (Kozleski, 2008, Langhout & Mitchell, 2008; Nuri-Robins et al., 2012; Wren, 1999).

TABLE 4.3: Aspects of the hidden curriculum

ASPECT	WHERE/WHAT	WHAT IS HIDDEN
Whole-school events	• Convocations, activities, or ceremonies (e.g., graduation, school play, field day)	• Expected behavior • Expected levels of participation
Rituals	• The school's motto, colors, etc.	• Historical context • Relationship of self to mascot
Rules	• School policies regarding homework, discipline, and safety (e.g., fire drills) • Appropriate behavior on and the reason for field trips	• Expected behavior
School structures	• Class schedules (e.g., block scheduling, movement from one class to another, the length of time for lunch) • Student recognition for outstanding conduct, grades, and other achievements	• Time allotted for instruction, eating, socializing • Identifying social group norms • Accepting praise for positive behavior (i.e., could be culturally inappropriate to receive praise for otherwise expected behaviors)

Langhout and Mitchell (2008) suggest using the hidden curriculum as an object of discovery to help move discussions away from blaming the achievement gap on students and/or teachers. When we combine the valuable information that comes from students' funds of knowledge with a deep investigation of the hidden curriculum through the eyes of the UDL framework, the learning environment takes one more step toward becoming barrier free.

▶ The UDL Connection

UDL defines the curriculum as goals, assessments, methods, and materials. In most U.S. schools, the curriculum is guided by standards. The goal of any lesson should articulate what the students will learn and/or experience, but it should be flexible about how the goal will be met. The assessment, formative or summative, measures achievement of the goal. The methods and materials build out the lesson, bringing in resources, experiences, and tools to meet the needs of variable learners, including CLD students and ELs. Exploring the idea of a hidden curriculum expands our definition of flexibility. Although the hidden curriculum maintains historical thinking, stating "That's the way it's always been done," UDL encourages flexibility and choice. UDL gives us a framework to help identify entrenched beliefs, norms, and values; bring them into the light of thoughtful scrutiny; and make purposeful change based on a new way of thinking.

REFLECTION Choose one guideline and a hypothetical lesson or the design of your environment. Review the aspects of the hidden curriculum and investigate how your chosen guideline could help you minimize its influence.

Implicit Bias

Implicit bias is the "automatic, often unconscious impact that stereotypic associations with racial and other groups can have on perceptions, judgments, decision-making, and behavior" (Smolkowski, Girvan, McIntosh, Nese, & Horner, 2016, p. 179). Although implicit bias stems from our unconscious mind, it still causes us to take action and affects us in all areas of life. In a study on implicit bias in education, van den Bergh, Denessen, Hornstra, Voeten, and Holland (2010) measured both the explicit and implicit biases of elementary school teachers as well as their academic expectations for their students.

The researchers collected information on students' ethnicity, gender, socioeconomic status, and standardized test scores. When they controlled for gender and socioeconomic status, the analysis showed that teachers' implicit biases predicted the extent of the achievement gap on standardized tests of the non-minority and minority ethnic students. Data also demonstrated teachers' lower expectations for their ethnic minority students.

Because implicit bias affects us outside of our conscious efforts, it can be challenging to identify and mediate. One way to look at your own implicit biases is to take *The Implicit Association Test* (Project Implicit, 2011). This online assessment investigates different types of implicit bias using the action of split-second decisions. Although the results can help individuals understand the impact implicit bias has on their own processing, moving away from implicit bias takes additional, conscious, continuous action. The creators of the assessment are straightforward in saying there isn't enough current research to say exactly how or when implicit biases can be reduced or eliminated, but they do suggest a focus on structured decision processes that keep implicit biases from operating (Project Implicit, 2011).

▶ Read All about It!

Want to read more about implicit bias? Check out "Understanding Implicit Bias: Understanding What Educators Should Know," at *https://www.aft.org/ae/winter2015-2016/staats*.

Structured decision processes are most easily identified in relation to behavior. Data collection around disciplinary referrals has received a lot of attention from researchers (McIntosh, Girvan, Horner, & Smolkowski, 2014; Smolkowski et al., 2016). To study this issue, McIntosh and colleagues (2014) proposed the Vulnerable Decision Points model and used it to focus on implicit bias such as office referrals for relatively minor incidents of unwanted behavior by students of color. Their research found a higher number of office discipline referrals for African American students during the first 90 minutes of the day, which they were able to link back to implicit racial bias. To reduce the effects of implicit bias, the researchers concluded that a proactive look at decision points within the data (e.g., the infraction, where it happened, date, when in the day it happened, the teacher who wrote up the behavior) and what punishment was delivered (e.g., suspension) helped teams look for patterns of implicit bias. Directly related to behavior, the researchers also suggested explicitly defining expected behaviors and using data (e.g., date, time) to design a "self-review routine" (p. 15) teachers can use prior to taking disciplinary action. Because this and other research shows how implicit bias interferes with how we support our students (Staats, 2016), it is crucial we acknowledge it and design with it in mind.

▶ The UDL Connection

When schools decide to establish more explicit expectations around behavior (e.g., defining what a positive behavior looks like and defining what would lead to an office disciplinary referral), students' behavioral outcomes improve (Bohanon et al., 2006). Defining the expectations, though, is just one piece. Those expectations need to be explicitly taught. Just as with any other topic or skill, students need to learn how and when to display certain behaviors. To ensure full access to this critical information, teachers should use UDL to design those lessons.

Second, planning deliberately using the UDL framework is a structured decision-making process. Whether you begin methods, materials, and assessments, or you use a tighter curriculum with embedded lessons, when you use the UDL framework to make design choices for variable learners, including CLD students and ELs, the structure of the framework guides your decision making. That said, we recommend proactively thinking about implicit bias, how it weaves its way into your lessons and learning environment, and how you can select strategies aligned with the UDL framework to reduce its impact. In addition, look for ways to collect student outcome data (academic or behavioral) and review it for patterns of potential bias across culture and race.

REFLECTION Return to a previous lesson. Examine the goal that was shared with your students and the assessments you designed, both formative and summative. In what ways did your assessment(s) align with the goal? In what ways did you assess other skills (e.g., spelling, grammar)? Did you provide specific feedback on effort and outcomes?

Stereotype Threat

Hundreds of studies over the course of twenty-plus years have clarified that stereotype threat exists (Taylor & Walton, 2011; Thoman, Smith, Brown, Chase, & Lee, 2013). We all belong to cultures and groups, and when we sense that belonging to that culture or group creates judgment or seemingly confirms our abilities (or lack of abilities), we experience stereotype threat. This literature helps us understand that our ELs and CLD students face stereotype threat daily, whether it is imposed on them or they self-interpret their abilities. As is the case with implicit bias, we do not always know we are affected by stereotype threat, whether we are the teacher or the student. Studies have linked stereotype threat to girls' lower achievement in math (Ganley et al., 2013; Galdi, Cadinu, & Tomasetto, 2014; Picho, 2016), students of color academically underperforming (Bruce, Getch, & Ziomek-Daigle, 2009; Rodríguez, 2014; Taylor & Walton, 2011), and research showing how stereotype threat can directly interfere with learning (Taylor & Walton, 2011). Each of these studies show that (1) stereotype threat can lead to decreased learning and performance, and (2) stereotype threat can have an adverse impact on motivation (Sansone & Smith, 2000; Sansone & Thoman, 2005; Thoman et al., 2013).

The UDL Connection

Stereotype threat affects both learning and the student's affective connection to the classroom. Some see Carol Dweck's work on growth mindset (2006) as a way to lessen stereotype threat among students (Viadero, 2007). Having a growth mindset encourages us to move away from a fixed mindset of intelligence. Instead of believing that a "smart" person already has the knowledge needed to succeed, a growth mindset leads us to understand that intelligence is acquired over time through failure and experience. The work of Dweck is embedded throughout the principle of engagement, though it plays out most through the guideline of options for self-regulation.

Other studies on stereotype threat focus on test taking and the anxiety linked to that task. Two ways you can use UDL to address that concern is (1) through the principle of engagement (options of self-regulation), and (2) paying close attention to the principle of action and expression, specifically the guideline of options for executive functions. As discussed in chapters 2 and 3, not all students will move through the act of planning and strategy development the same way due to cultural differences.

When you identify different pathways for students to travel and they can identify how to best improve on and grow their executive functions, there is a stronger possibility that they will be able to surpass stereotype threats they might have otherwise experienced.

Microaggressions

Microaggressions are unconscious and conscious actions that are either intentionally or unintentionally derogatory. These actions can be taken by students or educators. Comments ranging from a racial epithet or slur to comments like "You sure don't act Black," or "I thought all Asian kids were smart," or "Is that costume from your country?" are examples of microaggressions. Sue et al. (2007) defines the overall term of microaggressions as "brief and commonplace daily, verbal, behavioral, and environmental indignities, whether intentional or unintentional, that communicate hostile derogatory, or negative racial slights and insults to the target person or group" (p. 273).

▶ Read All about It!

Read more about microaggressions here: *www.apa.org/ monitor/2009/02/microaggression.aspx.*

Why are microaggressions so dangerous and why should educators be aware of them? They can emotionally undermine already marginalized or vulnerable students. When such negative statements happen in the learning environment, it can get in the way of learning (see more about how our affective networks are crucial to our learning in chapter 7).

How are microaggressions perpetrated? Because microaggressions can be so subtle, they might be considered part of everyday language. For example, in communities that have historically been White or segregated, how English is spoken by minority cultures can be devalued, leading to microaggressive comments (Ee, 2013; Henfield, 2011) such as, "Your English is so good!" or "That's not how we say that word around here." In both cases, the underlying intentional or unintentional message is "you don't belong," but because this is "the way it's always been" or "this is the way things work around here," there is resistance to change.

▶ The UDL Connection

Language is integral to communication, but not all students utilize the English language in the same way. Students' use of English can be based on their status as an EL, but it is also directly impacted by their community and home environment. The principle of representation gives us the most direct line to support our students' understanding and use of English. Microaggressions, though, make us think about how we communicate with our students. Assuming you want to provide positive and helpful feedback, one place to begin is to employ the guidelines of sustaining effort and persistence and examining mastery-oriented feedback. Providing mastery-oriented feedback requires thorough, directive comments based on the material and checking your students' use of feedback. For example, suppose after Sheila reads Tyrone's essay, she offers commentary focused on his work: "Reread where you listed several adjectives to describe the house. Did you place commas in the right places based on MLA?" Your follow-up praise can directly reflect on the student's work, helping to diminish the possibility of a microaggression.

Why do microaggressions challenge us? First, because these statements and actions exist within implicit biases, it can be difficult to recognize them. Second, microaggressions are a mix of the instigator, the recipient, and the context; they push emotional buttons;

and they are extremely difficult to separate from other dimensions, including oppression, power, and privilege (Sue et al., 2017). While researchers are working to identify specific solutions to diminish microaggressions, current suggestions include practical instruction about diversity (Ee, 2013), representing all present cultures within the curriculum and extracurricular events (Henfield, 2011), and raising awareness of microaggressions so perpetrators, often White, can identify and change their behaviors (Sue et al., 2007).

Conversations about Race

As stated by Coles-Ritchie and Smith (2017), "Race continues to be a major indicator for how schools are organized and who fares best within them" (p. 173). Disproportionality in outcomes still exists, and the deep conversations that address why inequities continue don't always occur. Many teachers view these conversations as too controversial, sensitive, or emotional (hooks, 1994), and they do not believe they have the skills necessary to constructively take part in this kind of discussion (Coles-Ritchie & Smith, 2017; Singleton & Linton, 2006). But purposeful conversations about race are a critical component in unearthing the hidden curriculum, implicit bias, and microaggressions as they relate to culture. Gay (2010) and other authors (Ladson-Billings in Singleton & Linton, 2006; Tatum, 1997) concur that sterilized conversations don't provide space for discomfort and conflict and do not lead to a critical analysis of social injustice.

Beverly Tatum provides some guidance in her powerful book *Why Are All the Black Kids Sitting Together in the Cafeteria: And Other Conversations about Race* (1997). Offering advice that is still relevant twenty years after it was published, Tatum addresses the complex issue of racism in the United States and has a chapter titled "Embracing a Cross-Dialogue." As she does throughout the book, she uses the voices of former students and workshop attendees to demonstrate the complexity of emotions, including fear, experienced during conversations about race and racism. In that vein of fear she writes:

"What if I make a mistake?" you may be thinking. "Racism is a volatile issue, and I don't want to say or do the wrong thing." In nearly twenty years of teaching and leading workshops about racism, I have made many mistakes. I have found that a sincere apology and a genuine desire to learn from one's mistakes are usually rewarded with forgiveness. If we want for perfection, we will never break the silence. The cycle of racism will continue uninterrupted. (p. 205)

To structure these conversations, Gay (2010) recommends "genuine, interethnic group dialogues" (p. 225). *Courageous Conversations about Race: A Field Guide to Achieving Equity in Schools* (Singleton & Linton, 2006) is one recognized method with accompanying materials. What is most important, though, is for educators to have the space, time, and facilitation necessary to establish open conversations about racism and cultural oppression and identify the steps they can take as a school community to support their students. These are not one-and-done meetings: these are conversations that move and shift over time (Gay, 2013). They will likely respond to the school culture and race and to what is happening locally and nationally related to culture and race. Even though these are conversations are often sidestepped because they are complex and can be uncomfortable, they are necessary to develop what Tatum (1997) refers to as a *cross-racial dialogue*.

▶ The UDL Connection

Gay (2013) shares that CRT is "an equal educational opportunity initiative that accepts differences among ethnic groups, individuals, and cultures as normative to the human condition and valuable to societal and personal development" (p. 50). CRT sees the differences across humans and society as the norm and not the exception. The UDL framework tells us that all learners are variable; it's how our brains work (see chapter 2). UDL sees learner variability as the constant, not the exception.

Consider this quote from Rose et al. (2013):

Regardless of age and across all cultures, a person changes dramatically over time, and even moment-to-moment as a function of context.... Importantly, this kind of individual variability is not limited to behavior: It is pervasive at every level of analysis, from minds..., to brains..., to genomes..., and to cells.... In each case, individual variability is the rule, not the exception....

The beginning of this quote tells us that the concept of variability needs to be added into conversations about race. We all learn differently based on the context. In schools, the context is the learning environment (because all spaces within a school should be used for learning). How we design the learning context determines what kind of access our students will have to learning. The impact of UDL can increase dramatically when we take into consideration the impact culture has on learning. Applying the suggestions given in chapter 3 and throughout the book that link UDL and Culturally Responsive Design will take you steps forward in your application of Culturally Responsive Teaching.

Designing culturally responsive environments requires us to think about how our own cultural background influences our teaching; designing those environments using UDL requires us to define what a learning environment is. Once we recognize that the environment includes the space in which learning takes place; the why, how, and when we're using spaces, resources, and strategies; and the relationships we have within that learning space, we can begin to see the impact the environment can have on the learner.

Culturally responsive environments designed using UDL accept that all students are variable, learning is based on context, all students can and should become expert learners, and accessibility also means responding to students' culture. We use our students' funds of knowledge (González et al., 2005) to inform our design, but we also look at our own funds of knowledge to see how they influence our design.

In this chapter, you read that hidden barriers can include the hidden curriculum (i.e., beliefs, norms, and values that don't align with a student's culture), implicit bias (i.e., often unconscious decisions and perceptions based on stereotypic associations), and microaggressions (i.e., unconscious and conscious actions that are intentionally or unintentionally derogatory). Although there are no clearly identified and fully researched solutions to these barriers, leaders in the field recommend deep and purposeful conversations about bias and race (Gay, 2010; Ladson-Billings in Singleton & Linton, 2006; Tatum, 1997), and we encourage you to keep these hidden barriers in mind when designing using the UDL framework. Ultimately, teachers who are involved in culturally responsive practices must be willing to observe these three tenets:

- Listen with the intent to learn.

- Implement with the intent to include.

- Reflect with the intent to grow.

REFLECTION QUESTIONS

1. How does the hidden curriculum impact your academic curriculum?

2. What implicit biases do you think you have, and how might you plan so they are not a barrier to your students' learning?

3. What microaggressions have you heard and how have they made you feel?

4. How can you support conversations about bias, race, and culture in your school?

5. What is a next step you will take in your classroom related to CRT?

CHECK-IN: UDL AND CRT

What hidden barriers are in your school? Use the following table to evaluate some aspects.

CHECK-IN: UDL AND CRT

ASPECT	WHERE/WHAT	HOW CAN IT BE UNHIDDEN?
Whole-school events	Convocations, assemblies, activities, or ceremonies (e.g., graduation, school play, field day)	
Rituals	The school's motto, colors, etc.	
Rules	School policies regarding homework, discipline, and safety (e.g., fire drills)	

PART II

Applying Culturally Responsive Design to Second- or Dual-Language Learning

Dual-Language Learning and UDL

This chapter focuses on stages of second language (L2) or dual-language learning and aspects of language acquisition that impact learner variability and expression, including executive functions, such as planning and organizing tasks, solving problems, and code switching.

Meet Mia

A middle school teacher with 15 years' experience, Mia loves teaching. Yet this year is really challenging. Nearly half of her students are ELs—all speaking different first languages. The good news is that most of them are making academic progress, except for Manny. He and his family arrived three months ago from a rural area of the Philippines, where his formal schooling was limited. According to his records, Manny's home language is Tagalog. But there is no assessment of his L1 verbal skills because none of the ESL teachers or interpreters speak Tagalog. Other than saying "Hi" and answering yes or no in English, he rarely speaks in class and seems to be in a constant state of confusion.

"Am I supposed to develop an individual program just for Manny?" Mia asks her principal. She then suggests that if Manny needs an individualized approach, he should be referred for a special education evaluation. "He's so far behind the other students. Maybe he has a language disability. He'll get the individual attention he needs in a special program," she explains.

DUAL-LANGUAGE LEARNING OR LEARNING DISABILITY?

Mia wants to refer Manny for a special education evaluation because he is not progressing as quickly as her other students and she believes that his academic and language difficulties could be the result of a disability. What Mia doesn't realize is that Manny's skills are common characteristics of ELs at his stage of L2 acquisition. He is a newcomer with limited formal schooling and exposure to English. As mentioned in chapter 2, learners' backgrounds, exposure to English, and history of formal schooling significantly impact the development of learner variability and L2 skills. More than likely, his language skills are still developing. (See Paradis, Genesee, and Crago [2011] for an extensive discussion of the differences between dual-language development and language impairment.)

What Manny needs most at this point is predictability, lots of practice, and scaffolds that gradually add more challenge. Predictability in classroom routines and performance expectations will address his affective learning needs (as discussed in chapter 7), thereby reducing his anxiety and confusion. Multiple opportunities to practice in an accepting environment will advance his L1 language acquisition exponentially, and scaffolds with graduated support for higher levels of performance will bolster his expressive dual-language skills.

STRATEGIC LEARNING AND DUAL-LANGUAGE SKILLS

Originating in the front part of the brain, the strategic networks operate like an air traffic control system for learners (Center on the Developing Child at Harvard University, 2011). They manage multiple incoming and outgoing neural patterns related to expression and executive function skills. As a neural unit, executive functions control how learners set and prioritize goals, analyze problems, make judgments, plan and organize tasks, and monitor their own learning. These functions include the following:

- Inhibitory control, which helps learners attend to tasks and ignore distractions

- Mental flexibility, which allows learners to switch gears, multitask, and explore innovative approaches

- Working memory, which controls short-term manipulation of information

Specifically, the strategic networks—particularly those controlling executive function skills—work with the affective and recognition networks to orchestrate second- or dual-language learning tasks, such as focusing on L2 input, evaluating it, determining its meaning, and formulating the learner's response. For example, figure 5.1. illustrates the many steps ELs might take to comprehend and respond during a second- or dual-language learning task. Adequate working memory is particularly vital for ELs because it permits dual-language learners to mentally juggle language input as they code-switch and translate. This process is explained in more detail later in this chapter.

Becoming a proficient bilingual or multilingual speaker can be a long-term process, but it has certain advantages. Results from recent brain research suggest that the neural networks involved with executive functions are more active in the brains of bilingual children (Willis, 2012).

FIGURE 5.1: Managing neural patterns and executive functions for expression
© ELI BROPHY, PHILADELPHIA, PA

STAGES OF LANGUAGE DEVELOPMENT

As ELs develop second- or dual-language proficiency, they typically progress through a series of stages. Understanding these stages will provide you with a backdrop for evaluating progress in second- or dual-language development among your ELs. Two commonly used sets of L2 stages of development are (1) the WIDA Consortium's six levels of English language development, and (2) Krashen and Terrell's five stages of L2 acquisition (cited in Hill & Miller, 2013).

WIDA Language Levels

The WIDA Consortium studies L2 development, creates resources for L2 instruction, and is used in nearly forty states. WIDA defines language development standards that measure steps of language acquisition process along a continuum (WIDA Consortium, 2012). The WIDA six levels of English language development are:

Level 1: Entering Learners understand common social utterances and single-word statements containing simple phrases and structures, such as Wh-questions. They use one-word and simple phrases and speak in *chunks* of language.

Level 2: Emerging Learners comprehend multiple related simple sentences and compound structures across content areas. Their emerging expression sounds formulaic, and includes short sentences, repetitive phrases, and general content vocabulary.

Level 3: Developing Learners comprehend discussions of content-related ideas, common idioms, and extended discourse expressed in compound and complex sentences. They demonstrate emerging expressive complexity using words with multiple meanings and specific content vocabulary in varying simple and compound sentences.

Level 4: Expanding Learners comprehend a variety of sentences, including complex sentences in connected discourse, expressions with multiple meanings, and technical content-related vocabulary. They speak with emerging cohesion in short, expanded, compound, and some complex sentences using specific and technical content vocabulary and idioms.

Level 5: Bridging Learners comprehend rich, descriptive discussions that contain a variety of complex sentences, technical and abstract content-related vocabulary, and shades of meaning. They express their ideas in cohesive, organized, and coherent ways using technical and abstract vocabulary in multiple complex sentences.

Level 6: Reaching Learners demonstrate automaticity, comprehend a range of age/grade-appropriate oral and written language, and use content-related language to access new information. Expression reflects age/grade-appropriate oral fluency, skillful interpersonal interaction, strategic use of academic language, and communication of content knowledge and ideas with precision and sophistication (WIDA Consortium, 2014).

▶ **Breaking News!**

The WIDA website hosts a plethora of resources here: *https://www.wida.us/.*

Five Stages of L2 Acquisition

Similar in some ways to how all children learn language, ELs tend to progress through stages of second-language acquisition in a sequential manner, as illustrated in figure 5.2. Hill and Miller (2013) adapted stages of second-language acquisition established by Krashen and Terrell in the 1980s. They describe five stages of L2 development:

Silent/Receptive or Preproduction Stage ELs may understand up to 500 English words, but they rarely speak. They use gestures and body language, and respond yes/no to simple questions.

Early Production Stage After about 6 months of exposure to English, ELs may understand up to 1,000 English words. In response to yes/

no and simple questions, they will use 1- or 2-word phrases, point, and nod. This stage can last up to 6 months to a year.

Speech Emergence Stage During this stage, ELs will understand 3,000 or more English words. They use phrases and sentences that contain grammatical and pronunciation errors but will likely have difficulty understanding abstract, sarcastic, and figurative language. This stage can last from 1 to 3 years.

Intermediate Language Fluency Stage During this stage, ELs will understand 6,000 or more English words. They will give their opinions and ask questions. They can write essays. Their use of complex sentences may contain a few grammatical errors. This stage can last from 3 to 5 years.

Advanced Language Proficiency This stage may be reached in 5 to 7 years after first exposure to English. At this point in their L2 development, ELs have near native English verbal capacity. They understand content vocabulary and can follow academic discussions. Their grammar and vocabulary usage is comparable to their non-EL peers.

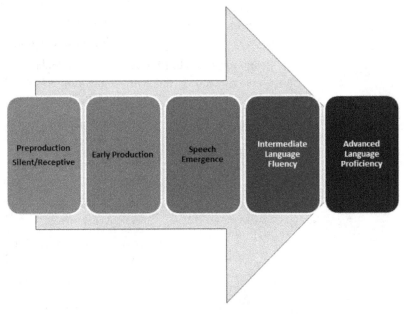

FIGURE 5.2: Stages of L2 development based on Hill and Miller (2013)

As discussed in earlier chapters, learning is shaped by experiences, language, and culture. These factors also influence how quickly ELs become proficient at L2. Considering linguistic variability, L2 learning will not necessarily advance in an orderly and systematic way. Although experts believe that developing English proficiency usually takes 5 to 7 years, some ELs who have limited formal schooling prior to their exposure to a second language may take as many as 10 years. However, knowledgeable educators can provide meaningful assistance to accelerate L2 advancement. See table 5.1 for examples of helpful strategies you can use to support second- or dual-language acquisition as ELs progress through the various L2 language stages.

TABLE 5.1: Example strategies for specific L2 language levels

L2 LANGUAGE STAGE	CHARACTERISTICS	EXAMPLES OF STRATEGIES
Silent/Receptive or Preproduction Exposure to L2 = 0 to 6 mos.	• Understand up to 500 L2 words • Understand almost no L2 academic vocabulary • Rarely speak; use gestures and body language • Respond yes/no to simple questions	• Offer welcoming environment with packet of lists of translated social greetings, survival language, common vocabulary/phrases • Post charts or visuals with common directions • Pair with L1 peer partners • Use visuals, manipulatives, real-life objects (realia), digital media • Use modeling and hands-on exercises • Adjust rate of speech as needed • Allow gestures, pointing, physical responses • Provide picture board for communication • Emphasize listening skills • Pre-teach core content vocabulary

L2 LANGUAGE STAGE	CHARACTERISTICS	EXAMPLES OF STRATEGIES
Early Production Exposure to L2 = 6 mos. to 1 yr.	• Understand ~1,000 L2 words • Understand limited L2 academic vocabulary • Respond yes/no and simple questions • Use 1- or 2-word phrases, point, nod • Possess basic interpersonal communication skills • Can copy words	• Simplify language without lowering expectations • Ask questions to elicit 1- or 2-word responses (e.g., who, which one, what, how many) • Pre-teach academic vocabulary using pictures and other visuals • Use choral reading • Provide opportunities for repetition and scaffolded practice • Pair with L1 peer partner • Focus on listening comprehension and receptive vocabulary
Speech Emergence Exposure to L2 = 1 to 3 yrs.	• Understand 3,000+ L2 words • Respond orally and in writing • Use phrases and sentences • Common grammatical and pronunciation errors • Difficulty understanding abstract, sarcastic, figurative language	• Review instructions step-by-step • Link to prior knowledge, cultural connections • Rephrase vocabulary; teach synonyms, antonyms • Use graphic organizers, such as Venn diagrams, T-charts, character perspective charts • Use short, engaging readings • Highlight critical features, patterns • Focus on describing, classifying, comparing, contrasting, summarizing, synthesizing

L2 LANGUAGE STAGE	CHARACTERISTICS	EXAMPLES OF STRATEGIES
Intermediate Language Fluency Exposure to L2 = 3 to 5 yrs.	• Understand 6,000+ L2 words • State opinions, ask questions, and use complex sentences • Write essays, connected narrative • Occasional grammatical errors • Function close to academic level of non-EL peers	• Use brainstorming tools, semantic webs • Ask how and why questions re: opinions, judgment, explanation • Teach abstract vocabulary, figurative language • Focus on evaluating and inferring • Use recorded books, video and audio-narrated resources • Guide reading of texts with key questions and skeletal outlines • Add challenge gradually
Advanced Language Proficiency Exposure to L2 = 5 to 7 yrs.	• Understand 12,000+ L2 vocabulary • Understand content vocabulary • Can follow academic discussions • Grammar and vocabulary usage comparable to non-EL peers • Capable of advanced academic language (CALP)	• Teach note-taking, journal skills • Teach study skills, test-taking skills

SOCIAL VS. ACADEMIC LANGUAGE ACQUISITION

Experts such as Cummins (1984) differentiate between development of social and academic language skills for ELs. Language skills used to socially interact with others, such as playing games and sports or on the playground with peers, are called Basic Interpersonal Communication Skills (BICS). Meaningfully connected to the social context, they can appear automatic because learning them requires little cognitive demand. They are typically the earliest utterances learned—usually within six months to two years after first exposure to L2. Proficiency at social language can be misinterpreted as L2 language competence. ELs who are dropped from ESL services as soon as they demonstrate social language proficiency will flounder in the classroom.

Cognitive Academic Language Proficiency (CALP) refers to formal academic learning, including listening, speaking, reading, and writing about subject area content material. CALP skills are closely associated with the learner's ability to perform academic tasks such as comparing, classifying, synthesizing, analyzing, and inferring. ELs may take from five to seven years to develop CALP proficiency.

▶ Assumptions Can Be Misleading

A very talkative girl, Makayla readily spoke with everyone, asking questions, giving her opinions, and sharing weekend plans of shopping and going to parties. Her teacher Bill questioned why she was still receiving ESL services, thinking that it was just an opportunity to get out of class. Makayla wasn't doing well academically but Bill felt it was due to a lack of effort. When he checked her language proficiency scores, he was shocked to discover that her listening, reading, and writing skills were all significantly below grade level. He realized that Makayla continued to need ESL services and that she needed far more academic assistance than he was providing.

Makayla's case illustrates how assumptions about language competence based solely on oral performance can be misleading. Contrary to appearances, oral fluency does not equal proficiency in understanding, speaking, reading, and writing. If a learner can speak or read fluently, it does not automatically mean that he comprehends what he is saying or reading.

MULTIPLE MEANS OF ACTION AND EXPRESSION

The UDL principle of Action and Expression undergirds the development of second- or dual-language skills in ELs. Note the intensive focus on expressive language skills listed under the UDL principle of Action and Expression in figure 5.3.

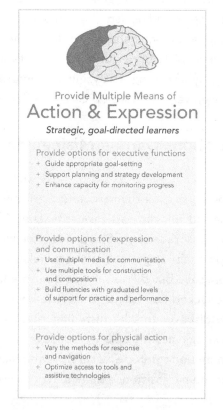

Provide Multiple Means of
Action & Expression
Strategic, goal-directed learners

Provide options for executive functions
+ Guide appropriate goal-setting
+ Support planning and strategy development
+ Enhance capacity for monitoring progress

Provide options for expression
and communication
+ Use multiple media for communication
+ Use multiple tools for construction
  and composition
+ Build fluencies with graduated levels
  of support for practice and performance

Provide options for physical action
+ Vary the methods for response
  and navigation
+ Optimize access to tools and
  assistive technologies

FIGURE 5.3: UDL Guidelines for Action and Expression 2014 CAST, INC. USED WITH PERMISSION.

Applying the UDL principle of Action and Expression for ELs involves presenting a multitude of options for expression, including translated and bilingual alternatives and providing numerous opportunities for meaningful practice and appropriate feedback. In addition, a culturally responsive learning environment engages learners in active learning with options for movement and response, and scaffolds for developing planning, organizing, and executive function skills. See table 5.2 for specific examples of UDL strategies that support second- or dual-language development.

TABLE 5.2: Examples of effective strategies aligned with UDL Action and Expression Guidelines

UDL GUIDELINES FOR ACTION AND EXPRESSION	STRATEGY EXAMPLES
Provide options for physical action • Vary the methods for response and navigation • Optimize access to tools and assistive technologies	• Provide options for responding, e.g., verbal, written, illustration, miming, physical model, technology, music, dance/movement, visual art or video • Engage learners in active learning and movement, e.g., movement from one center to another, stand when you have the answer, ball toss to ask or answer questions, 4-corners exercise, thumbs up/thumbs down for comprehensive check

UDL GUIDELINES FOR ACTION AND EXPRESSION	STRATEGY EXAMPLES
Provide options for expression and communication • Use multiple media for communication • Use multiple tools for construction and composition • Build fluencies with graduated levels of support for practice and performance	• Teach learners to use multiple modes to present information, e.g., text, slides, video, realia, drawings/ images • Encourage learners to complement verbal presentations and written narratives with digital versions, video, pictures • Encourage learners to paraphrase directions, responses, content • Allow learners to use social media and interactive web tools, e.g., discussion forums, chats, storyboards, comic strips, animation • Allow learners a choice of production media, e.g., point, draw, demonstration, text, oral/speech, illustration, comics, storyboards, music, visual art, video • Offer choices of types of tools to create products, e.g., paper-pencil, laptop, wiki, Promethean board, whiteboard, manipulatives (such as blocks, base-ten blocks, 3D models) • Provide spell checkers, grammar checkers, word prediction software, text-to-speech (TTS) software, dictation, audio recording • Offer scaffolds for assignments, then gradually remove them as performance levels improve • Use literary circles and similar peer-to-peer partnering

UDL GUIDELINES FOR ACTION AND EXPRESSION	STRATEGY EXAMPLES
Provide options for executive functions • Guide appropriate goal-setting • Support planning and strategy development • Enhance capacity for monitoring progress	• Encourage learners to develop and monitor personal learning goals • Teach learners to use diaries, journals, progress charts • Provide sentence starters, sentence strips, answer stems • Use semantic webbing, story webs, outlining tools, concept mapping tools • Use guided questions for comprehending complex texts

Scaffolds

Although chapter 7 contains a robust discussion of scaffolds and their use, a brief explanation related to the UDL principle of Action and Expression is warranted here. Scaffolds are temporary assistance or supportive strategies that can be gradually removed as skills and performance improve. Scaffolds for executive function and expressive skills include planning and organizing tools, such as these:

• Outlining strategies

• Concept mapping, semantic webbing, and story webs

• Sentence starters and sentence strips

• Facilitated reading guides that use guided questions and answer stems for comprehending complex texts

• Calendars, diaries, journals, and progress charts

Gradual Release of Responsibility (GRR)

A successful method of building student ownership of learning is GRR, or the gradual release of responsibility. GRR shifts the responsibility of performing a task from the teacher to the student over time (Fisher, 2008; Pearson & Gallagher, 1983). It is especially effective when it is embedded in your scaffolds. For instance, middle school science teacher Gabriel often uses *think-alouds,* talking about each step he takes as he demonstrates how to complete a new science experiment. He phases these *think-alouds* out as the students become more adept at conducting specific types of experiments. In another example, Destiny, a sixth-grade mathematics teacher, routinely employs an "I do it—We do it—You do it together—You do it alone" sequence for teaching advanced mathematics with her class. This sequence builds learner independence. A librarian, Sheila frequently refers to the anchor charts modeling the steps for research that are displayed on the library walls as guides for students. As learners become more proficient at research techniques, they refer to the anchor charts less often. These examples illustrate easy ways to infuse GRR strategies that build student ownership into your instructional practice.

Expression Options

The UDL principle of Action and Expression encourages teachers to offer multiple options for expression. In addition to oral and written narratives, all learners, including ELs, should have choices, such as slides, posters, video, realia, models, manipulative, drawings, pantomime, animation, music, visuals, and pictorial images. Choral reading or recitation can help ELs develop appropriate speech rhythm, intonation, and prosody.

Opportunities to Practice

Opportunities to practice L2 skills do not have to dominate your lesson planning. In fact, inconspicuous opportunities for practicing L2 expressive skills can be infused into your instructional methods. For instance, ELs at earlier stages of L2 development can repeat or paraphrase directions to check their comprehension. For older learners, guided use of social media and interactive digital tools (e.g., discussion forums, backchannel chats and other digital discussion tools, and storyboards) offer opportunities for practice in an engaging context.

Feedback on Developing L2 Skills

While ELs are still developing L2, feedback should focus on content rather than production, especially for those learners at earlier stages of L2 development. It's important to offer models of accurate spelling and sentence structure. Spell checkers, grammar checkers, and word prediction software are helpful self-correction tools. However, redlining written assignments and correcting every verbal utterance interrupts the flow of students' thinking and can cause unwarranted anxiety (Lenski & Verbruggen, 2010). Rather than repeated direct correction, identify a few specific errors that the student is close to learning. If possible, conduct an error analysis to determine which structures are most responsive to reminders. React first to the content of verbalizations, and then restate the learner's incorrect statements using correct models. For instance, when Diego says "No music in box," Nicole, an elementary music teacher, replies, "There are no music instruments in the box?" In this way, Diego knows he was understood. Instead of stopping the class to ask Diego to repeat the utterance correctly, Nicole provides him with the correct English syntax as a model. In this way, Nicole lets Diego know he was understood and provides him with the correct English syntax as a model. This approach encourages self-correction.

In summary, to address learning through the strategic networks, teachers should provide multiple means of action and expression. Culturally Responsive Design strategies include offering culturally responsive scaffolds used with GRR, and providing appropriate culturally responsive tools for planning, organizing, expression, and practice. Remember that it's important to allow ELs sufficient time and support to develop their L2 language proficiency because false assumptions about L2 development can lead to premature, incorrect judgments about student performance.

REFLECTION QUESTIONS

1. How is acquisition of a second language different from learning a first language?

2. What's surprising to you about the strategic networks?

3. How might linguistic variability be misinterpreted as a disability?

4. How could an English-only learning environment be enabling for ELs? How could it be disabling?

5. In what ways can you strengthen your learners' working memory?

CHECK-IN: 3-2-1 QUESTIONS ABOUT ACTION AND EXPRESSION FOR CLD STUDENTS/ELS AND YOUR INSTRUCTION

A. What are three steps you can take immediately to enhance the expressive skills of CLDs?

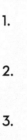

    1.

    2.

    3.

B. What two strategies can you adopt to improve the executive function skills for CLD students?

    1.

    2.

C. What one fact about CLD students and ELs do you know now that you didn't know before?

    1.

6

Culturally Responsive Representation

This chapter explains the importance of the recognition network—the parts of the brain involved in perception and comprehension—in learning English as a second language (L2). It highlights strategies to support language development, such as explicit teaching of vocabulary and offering scaffolds.

Meet Luis

When most of the students in Luis's elementary English as a second language (ESL) classes spoke Spanish as their first language (L1), lesson development was straightforward. As a bilingual speaker, he could offer the Spanish translation whenever needed. It was relatively easy for him to link meaning with what learners already knew. Now, the ELs in his ESL classes speak over 50 different languages and are from all over the world, including China, Haiti, India, Iraq, Philippines, Somalia, Syria, South Korea, Ukraine, and Vietnam. Many of the newcomers to the United States had limited exposure to academics in their native countries or their schooling was repeatedly interrupted as they moved to and from refugee camps.

Luis realized that offering instantaneous translations is no longer a reliable strategy. One day, he asks fellow teacher Liz how she supports English development when students have such varied backgrounds. "My students have so much to learn and so little time to do it!" he says. "I need a new approach." A UDL expert, Liz encourages Luis to learn more about how to apply UDL to his lesson design, starting with the UDL principle of Representation.

Luis learns that the UDL framework guides educators to attend to learner variability across three sets of brain networks by applying three UDL principles. His immediate concern—developing L2 vocabulary skills—is primarily addressed by the recognition networks. Originating in the back of the brain, the recognition networks constantly sense and perceive stimuli in the environment; identify and assign meaning to what we see, hear, taste, smell, and touch; and transform it into usable, retrievable knowledge (Meyer, Rose, & Gordon, 2014). The recognition networks are critically important for accessing, understanding, and building language comprehension skills.

As discussed in chapter 2, recognition networks vary significantly from learner to learner because they are created in response to an individual's experiences and are shaped by language and culture. ELs also vary in how they understand vocabulary, symbols, and language structures in both L1 and L2. Consequently, effective teaching strategies need to be as flexible as they are supportive. If ELs are to make academic progress, every teacher, including content area teachers, must address L2 acquisition. In particular, all teachers need to explicitly teach academic vocabulary. UDL representation strategies and culturally responsive instruction can go hand-in-hand. For example, by offering culturally responsive scaffolds and providing appropriate translated materials and media, teachers help ELs connect their background and experiences with academic content, and construct deep understanding.

MULTIPLE MEANS OF REPRESENTATION

The UDL principle that addresses the recognition networks calls for providing multiple means of representation. Note the emphasis on developing language comprehension skills in the UDL Guidelines under the UDL principle of Representation in figure 6.1. Culturally Responsive Design aligned with UDL provides options for learners that assist with perception of various forms of information, including culturally responsive models, examples, nonlinguistic representations, multimedia, and assistive technologies, as needed.

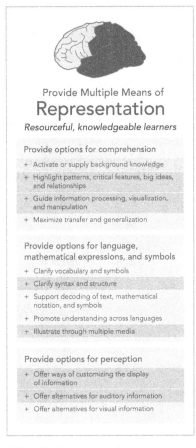

FIGURE 6.1: UDL Guidelines for Representation ©2014 CAST, INC. USED WITH PERMISSION.

In addition, culturally responsive instruction facilitates comprehension of language, mathematical expressions, and symbols by offering culturally responsive scaffolds; explicitly teaching academic vocabulary; and making translated materials and media available, such as bilingual dictionaries and texts, thus connecting new content with ELs' background and experiences. Table 6.1 includes additional examples of instructional CRT strategies aligned with the UDL Guidelines for Representation.

TABLE 6.1: Examples of effective culturally responsive instructional strategies aligned with the UDL Guidelines for Representation

UDL GUIDELINES FOR REPRESENTATION	STRATEGY EXAMPLES
Provide options for perception • Offer ways of customizing the display of information • Offer alternatives for auditory information • Offer alternatives for visual information	• Use nonlinguistic representations • Enlarge text to display on overhead • Provide assistive technologies, as needed, e.g., text-to-speech, speech-to- text, switch or adapted keyboard, screen reader, or word prediction • Use graphic novels vs. traditional literature • Use short, engaging, issue-based nonfiction readings

UDL GUIDELINES FOR REPRESENTATION	STRATEGY EXAMPLES
Provide options for language, mathematical expressions, and symbols • Clarify vocabulary and symbols • Clarify syntax and structure • Support decoding of text, mathematical notation, and symbols • Promote understanding across languages • Illustrate through multiple media	• Teach high-frequency academic vocabulary • Use think-aloud protocols to teach how to decode and analyze text, e.g., *See it—say it—repeat it* strategy • Use graphic organizers to relay associations • Teach words as parts of speech, give examples in sentences • Teach vocabulary as synonyms or cognates (i.e., words that are associated or similar in meaning, spelling, pronunciation in L1) • Use sentence frames, sentence starters • Model comprehension strategies, e.g., predicting, summarizing, evaluating, inferencing • Provide opportunities to apply new vocabulary in speaking, writing • Offer bilingual dictionaries, have learners make personal dictionaries • Post names of classroom items around the room in bilingual pairs • Illustrate with digital tools (software and hardware), e.g., document camera, digital camera, tablet, iPad, iPod, interactive whiteboard

UDL GUIDELINES FOR REPRESENTATION	STRATEGY EXAMPLES
Provide options for comprehension • Activate or supply background knowledge • Highlight patterns, critical features, big ideas, and relationships • Guide information processing, visualization, and manipulation • Maximize transfer and generalization	• Use K-W-L to activate background knowledge: What do you *know*; what do you *want* to learn; what did you *learn* • Make meaningful connections between content and student experiences • Build background knowledge by showing short videos or films (5–10 minutes) without dialogue • Complete story maps, story organizers, character perspective charts • Model processing using think-aloud protocols • Follow modeling/think-aloud protocols with opportunities for group and independent practice • Use a reading club, chat room, blogs, postings on class website • Use assignments that provide opportunities to synthesize learning via presentations, written reflections and analyses, Socratic seminars

Every Teacher Needs to Focus on Language

Just because a learner can read a word doesn't mean he comprehends its meaning. ELs require explicit teaching of content vocabulary, academic language, and sentence structures. Luis accepts his responsibility as an ESL teacher to assist ELs in developing L2 competency. He also realizes that since it can take a long time to reach language proficiency (more than seven years for some students), he can't be the only one teaching vocabulary to ELs. To effectively enhance language learning, every teacher, including those who teach content areas, needs to focus on L2 acquisition, particularly vocabulary development.

Construct Deep Understanding

Language learning, especially vocabulary learning, is enhanced when students are able to link new information with what they already know. This connection is particularly true for CLD students and ELs. Teachers need to offer specific opportunities to relate learners' prior knowledge with academic content. For instance, Jasmine starts each new unit with a K-W-L exercise that allows learners to activate background knowledge and connect their experiences and word knowledge with the new content. Likewise, Sebastian asks students to brainstorm and create word walls before the class begins reading a new book.

To apply the UDL principle of Representation to the development of L2 vocabulary knowledge and comprehension skills, use strategies that involve constructing deep understanding such as highlighting similarities and differences (e.g., comparing and contrasting), classification, and story and concept mapping. Identify key vocabulary words in content areas (such as science, social studies, mathematics), and then use them as a base to build more abstract concepts. Another useful tool is pairing language learning with movement and music, and using a variety of materials and media to represent language concepts, including manipulatives, nonlinguistic cues and prompts (such as pointing, gesturing, and matching objects to pictures), models, pictures, drawings, illustrations, videos, and pictographs (Hill & Miller, 2013). See table 6.2 for additional examples of materials and media content teachers can use to develop L2 proficiency.

> **REFLECTION** Most teachers represent content using a variety of materials and media. Which materials/media do you think are most effective for ELs?

TABLE 6.2: Examples of materials and media for developing L2 proficiency in content areas

EARLY CHILDHOOD	ENGLISH LANGUAGE ARTS	MATHEMATICS
• Real-life objects (realia) • Manipulatives • Pictures and photographs • Sequence story pictures • Illustrations, diagrams, and drawings • Animated video clips • Clay • Building tools/ LEGOs • Stamp sets • Books on tape • Picture library • Felt or magnetic figures of story elements • Hand puppets • Props for role-play • Tactile learning resources • Sorting games/ puzzles	• Graphic organizers • Word/phrase walls • Felt or magnetic story characters • Sequence story pictures • Posters or displays • Bulletin boards • Photographs • Cartoons/story maps • Audio books • Illustrations, diagrams, and drawings • Magazines/ newspapers • Videos and films • MP3 player/CD player • Journals/notebooks • Materials for projects • Picture slides • IPads/laptops/ audio recorders/ smartphones	• Graphic organizers • Blocks/cubes • Number lines • Counters/coins • Calculators • Protractors • Rulers, yard/meter sticks • Calendars • Clocks/sundials • Models and figures • Math board games • Digital math games

ARTS/PHYSICAL EDUCATION	SOCIAL STUDIES	SCIENCE
• Art material/tape/glue	• Graphic organizers	• Graphic organizers
• Materials for projects	• Charts/graphs	• Scientific instruments
• Clay	• Tables	• Measurement tools
• MP3 player/CD player	• Timelines	• Physical models
• Keyboard, musical instruments	• Geoboards	• Natural materials
• Manipulatives	• Geotracking	• Real substances/chemicals,
• Camera	• Maps	• Organisms or objects
• Sports equipment	• Globes	• Posters/Illustrations of processes or cycles
• IPads/laptops/audio recorders/smartphones	• Atlases	• Models and figures
	• Compasses	• Binoculars, cameras
	• Multicultural artifacts	• Books about nature/environment
	• Aerial and satellite photographs	• Mind-mapping software
	• Videos & films	
	• TV broadcasts/podcasts	
	• Picture slides	

Explicitly Teach Vocabulary

To promote L2 acquisition, Luis must explicitly teach academic vocabulary. He puts aside the stale ESL workbooks he's been using, dissects the vocabulary that students need to understand in their content classes, and develops new lessons that build on the school's academic curriculum.

One advantageous approach is to teach vocabulary using the three-tiered vocabulary system described by Beck, McKeown, & Kucan (2002). Vocabulary is organized by frequency of use and complexity:

Tier 1 Basic or common words or phrases that do not require explanations (e.g., color words, school and common items).

Tier 2 Frequent words or phrases that need explanation and are used often in various contexts and in a variety of academic texts. Tier 2 vocabulary includes more descriptive or precise words than Tier 1 vocabulary (e.g., pleased vs. happy) and linking words (e.g., so, at, if, then, because).

Tier 3 Academic vocabulary—words or phrases that are not common, that are specialized, or that are limited to a specific context and are not likely to be used outside the classroom (e.g., photosynthesis, revolutionary, equation).

Tier 2 and Tier 3 vocabulary emerge from a foundation of Tier 1 words. To differentiate for groups of ELs who are at varied L2 proficiency levels, teachers can define vocabulary from all three tiers to teach in every lesson. In this way, all learners can participate in the lesson. For example, for her lesson on *Alice in Wonderland*, Kelly identifies:

- Tier 1 words for the ELs at beginning L2 levels (e.g., red, white, up, down, cat, mouse, hat, key, drink, eat)

- Tier 2 vocabulary for the ELs at emerging and developing L2 levels (e.g., queen, king, hearts, rabbit, hare, caterpillar, adventure, tea, pocket watch, mad, unhappy, grin, grow, bored, curious)

- Tier 3 concepts for ELs at or near L2 proficiency (e.g., fantasy genre, nonsense, morals).

Build Multi-Literacies

All of the four language domains (i.e., listening, speaking, reading, and writing) are important to L2 acquisition and require specific attention. However, these two domains are essential:

- *listening*, because it requires learners to process information and understand the primary mode of instruction (i.e., verbalizations)

- *reading*, because it requires learners to process, comprehend, and interpret a fundamental source of learning content (i.e., written symbols and text)

To hasten academic progress, the four language domains must not be taught in a vacuum. As stated earlier, language learning is deeply braided within context and culture and embedded in social, cultural, and personal identity. Teachers should purposefully plan to build multi-literacies through frequent, specific opportunities to practice skills in listening, speaking, reading, and writing (New London Group, 1996). For instance:

- Latonya offers learners opportunities for *situated practice* that attends to learners' affective and recognition networks by immersing students in new content connected with what they already know (i.e., guided language learning within authentic contexts).

- Carol provides learners with opportunities for *overt instruction*, a meta-cognitive approach that activates the recognition networks and teaches students how to deconstruct language based on individual learner needs (i.e., conscious awareness of the code, patterns, and features of language).

- Sejei develops his social studies lessons within a *cultural and social frame* that engages the affective and recognition networks by linking content with relevant community, cultural, and valued-centered contexts (i.e., meaning-making within real-world environments).

- Avril uses *transformed practice*, which encourages learners to use their strategic networks to problem-solve and apply their new learning to real-world, culturally relevant contexts (i.e., problem-based and case-based learning).

Scaffolds

Comparable to scaffolds constructed around buildings that are undergoing renovation, instructional scaffolds are temporary assistance that bridge gaps between what the learner knows or can do and new knowledge and skills. The term was first used by Wood, Bruner, and Ross (1976), who described it as a process "that enables a child or novice to solve a task or achieve a goal that would be beyond his unassisted efforts" (p. 90). Vygotsky (1978) discussed the concept when he described a learner's zone of proximal development (ZPD) as the difference between what a learner can do alone and what she can do with assistance. Scaffolds may be used in a single situation to bridge the ZPD, or as a part of a fading process that gradually releases and transfers responsibility for task completion from the teacher to the student (i.e., gradual release of responsibility; see chapter 5 for a complete description).

Commonly used scaffolds include chunking information into meaningful, memorable bits that engage strategic networks by utilizing learners' working memories to process and transfer new content to long-term memory. Chunking is an effective way for ELs to remember and recall content in L2. Graphic organizers, semantic maps or webs, and story maps help organize the new content into memorable chunks. Also, sectioning reading passages into smaller portions reduces the possibility of ELs feeling overwhelmed by large segments of L2 text.

In general, instructional scaffolds are:

- *Content or conceptual scaffolds* that guide understanding of key concepts

- *Procedural or task scaffolds* that facilitate the effective use of appropriate tools and resources to complete a specific task (e.g., modeling, small group-instruction, peer-assisted activities)

- *Strategic scaffolds* that help students solve problems by employing alternative strategies and methods (e.g., graphic organizers)

- *Metacognitive scaffolds* that assist learners in making decisions about their own learning by prompting them to reflect and complete self-assessments (e.g., paraphrasing, think-alouds)

Infuse Scaffolds into Instructional Strategies

Often teachers use instructional strategies that naturally scaffold learning. For example:

- Elena teaches her students to generate questions while reading complicated content.

- Joaquin asks learners to annotate segments of their text as they are reading.

- Terry assigns note-taking during lectures as a graded assignment that is shared with the rest of the class.

- Marie provides anticipation guides for each unit to enlist prior knowledge and facilitate comprehension.

Another scaffold, deliberate reflection during a learning task, gives students time to translate, analyze, and/or synthesize new information. Research suggests that allowing learners to periodically *pause and reflect* for 3–5 seconds during a lecture or presentation will result in higher retention of subject matter (Braun & Simpson, 2004). Likewise, brief (3–5 minutes) opportunities to discuss content, such as think-pair-share or ping-pong discussions, helps ELs and others build context and meaning. Table 6.3 illustrates examples of scaffolds and suggested ways teachers can use them.

TABLE 6.3: Examples of scaffolds and ways to use them

SCAFFOLD	INSTRUCTIONAL USE
Advanced organizers	Present new information in a way that aids understanding; e.g.: • Venn diagrams: compare/contrast information • T-charts: compare two items/concepts, factual vs. complex questions • Concept ladder: shows levels of understanding from concrete to abstract • Flow charts: illustrate processes, cause and effect, decision making • Outlines: represent content in organized manner, e.g., frame • Organizational charts: illustrate hierarchies, decision making • Problem-solving charts: organizes problem-solving strategies, e.g., 5Ws • Gathering grid: collects data for analysis • Fishbone charts: guides writing, analyzing main ideas • Question matrix: facilitates framing arguments/predictions/questions • Timeline: presents information connected over time • Mnemonics: assists recall of details/data • Rubrics: defines expectations • V Diagram

SCAFFOLD	INSTRUCTIONAL USE
Concept maps	Organize or display relationships between concepts, for example: • Spider map • Hierarchal/chronological map • Systems map • Mind map
Examples	Display samples, realia (real objects), specimens, or illustrations to represent information.
Prompts	Aid recall of prior information or knowledge; e.g.: • Physical: body movements such as pointing, nodding, eye blinking, finger or foot tapping • Verbal/audio-recording: words/statements, such as "Go," "Stop," "What's next?", "Tell me how..." • Positional: place materials in a specific area or location to prompt student to act
Explanations	• Present and explain new content using written instructions, verbal explanations, visual images, videos, animation, audio files. • Omit extraneous details and focus on key vocabulary and core demand.
Choral responses	• Use rhymes, songs, or music/movement routines to assist with comprehension of details, essential facts, or complex information. • Consider using ethnic rhythms or L1 vocabulary.
Modeling	Demonstrate desired behavior or hands-on task, e.g., science experiment, art construction or performance; learners independently conduct task after model.

SCAFFOLD	INSTRUCTIONAL USE
Worked example	Demonstrate a complex problem and solution in a step-by-step manner, e.g., mathematics or science problem. A worked example usually includes: • Problem formation: introduction of principle or theory • Step-by-step example: demonstration of solution process • Solution practice: learner develops solutions to problem statements, independently or in pairs
Cue cards	Provide cards containing key words, phrases, or stem sentences to assist learners to recall specific vocabulary, concepts, problem-solving steps, or points to consider in a discussion.
Note-taking template/outlines	Provide worksheets, templates, or outlines to guide or organize student note taking.
Verbal Hints	Offer suggestions, cues, mnemonics, or acronyms, particularly for steps in a process, or to recall details; e.g., "Water then acid: Add the water and then the acid." "In 1492, Columbus sailed the ocean blue." "I before e except after c or when sounding like a in neighbor and weigh." PEMDAS = sequence to solving math equations: **P**arenthesis, **E**xponents, **M**ultiplication, **D**ivision, **A**ddition, **S**ubtraction.
Visual Cues	Use colored markers, pointing, or gestures to highlight information.
Question Cards/Stems	Provide cards containing content-specific questions about a topic or content, or incomplete sentences to stimulate thinking.
Stories	Stories can be used to inspire and motivate learners, particularly legends and stories steeped in students' cultural experiences. They explain complex and abstract material by referencing situations familiar to students.

SCAFFOLD	INSTRUCTIONAL USE
Chapter/unit or anticipation guides	Provide written guides highlighting key concepts, vocabulary, and questions to assist learning.
Notebooks	Offer a physical or digital notebook to help learners organize course material. It can include a class calendar, rubrics and explanations of assignments, a section for class notes, graphic organizers, tables, charts, and models.

Using Translation

Luis found that providing translation in Spanish was successful when his students were primarily Spanish-speaking. As the makeup of his class changed, translations became less practical. However, with digital translation tools and more bilingual texts available, teachers can use translations to support L2 development and content instruction even in classes of ELs with very diverse linguistic backgrounds. Keep the following in mind:

- ELs who can read in their L1 can use bilingual dictionaries, audio translation apps, and bilingual texts.

- ELs who cannot read in their L1 but have a strong aural L1 base can use multimedia and audio translations.

- ELs who do not demonstrate proficiency in their L1 will not benefit from translations or translated materials.

In summary, the UDL principle of Representation is crucial to developing L2 vocabulary skills and essential for building language comprehension skills. By offering culturally responsive scaffolds and providing translated materials and media, teachers help ELs connect their backgrounds and experiences to academic content and construct deep understanding. If every teacher, including content area teachers, addressed L2 acquisition by explicitly teaching academic vocabulary, ELs would make significant linguistic and academic progress.

REFLECTION QUESTIONS

How culturally responsive are the materials, and media that you use?

1. In what ways can learners engage in selecting representations that are culturally responsive?

2. How do you think the instruction of content teachers might change when they explicitly teach academic vocabulary, listening, and reading skills to ELs?

3. To what extent have you used instructional scaffolds? How successful have they been?

4. Scaffolds are temporary and are meant to be removed as learners progress. What would you do if learners seemed to be relying on scaffolds that you didn't think they needed?

CHECK-IN: HOW DO YOU REPRESENT VOCABULARY AND CONTENT FOR LEARNERS?

Brainstorm what culturally responsive representation of vocabulary and content looks like based on UDL and CRT strategies. Then, using a 0–3 scale, rate your representation strategies (0 = never; 1 = occasionally; 2 = often; 3 = always).

CHECK-IN: HOW DO YOU REPRESENT VOCABULARY AND CONTEXT FOR LEARNERS?

UDL AND CRT REPRESENTATION STRATEGIES	RATING
1.	O 1 2 3
2.	O 1 2 3
3.	O 1 2 3
4.	O 1 2 3
5.	O 1 2 3
6.	O 1 2 3
7.	O 1 2 3
8.	O 1 2 3
9.	O 1 2 3
10.	O 1 2 3

Context Matters

This chapter discusses how the affective networks shape learning and how the UDL principle of Engagement addresses cultural and linguistic variability, particularly by attending to context, balancing demands with resources, and encouraging a growth mindset.

Meet Tomás

Recognized as an excellent high school social studies teacher, Tomás introduces new units with intriguing verbal stories about the experiences of real people—usually teenagers—who lived during each time in history. Storytelling is a great hook for most of his students, but not all. He notices that some of the ELs look disinterested, or even bored. One day after class, Tomás approaches Fatima, who yawned throughout his story about teenage experiences during the U.S. Civil War. "I see you're tired today, Fatima. Didn't you get enough sleep last night?" he asked. She apologized for yawning during his lecture, said she slept fine, and then offered a blunt, unexpected comment: "Listening to English is hard work. I get tired." Tomás suddenly realizes that what appears to be boredom is language fatigue due to the physical stress of attending to and translating long verbal English passages.

DOUBLE-DUTY LEARNING

Raised in more than one culture, ELs are learning both the new language and the norms of the new culture. In the learning environment, they rely on the L2 to learn academics. Depending on their stage of L2 development, the demands of translating as well as learning academics requires intense focus. This is particularly true for ELs in middle and high school, especially those who are recent school entrants. Not only are they attempting to master complex subject matter, but they are simultaneously learning the norms of a new school environment. Literacy development can be very difficult for middle and high school newcomers. They have fewer years to develop the L2, and entry-level literacy instruction is often less available at the secondary level (Short & Fitzsimmons, 2007).

This was Fatima's issue. She was interested in Tomas's stories of teenage lives during the Civil War but was unable to sustain her listening and translating efforts. The learning environment offered no resources to match the demanding task of simultaneously listening and translating—no visuals, glossary, bilingual dictionary, or mind breaks. As a result, she grew fatigued and yawned.

Both boredom and fatigue are associated with an emotional response to the learning situation. In actuality, learning is primarily emotional work (Meacham, 2014). Originating from the mid-portion of the brain, the affective networks manage emotions and are critical for learners' emotional response to the learning environment. They are responsible for recruiting and sustaining interest, coping and persisting in the face of learning challenges, and maintaining motivation. Emotions vary and can include feelings of anxiety, hyper-excitement, discomfort, frustration, and stress within the learning environment.

According to Immordino-Yang and Damasio (2007), "humans are fundamentally emotional and social creatures" (p. 116). Every learning environment is associated with an emotional and social landscape that impacts how learners attend, inhibit distractions, set priorities, cope with stress, and persist against barriers (Meyer, Rose, & Gordon, 2014). The affective networks are built with every experience.

Likewise, every learning experience is associated with an emotional response. Some experiences are intense and evoke a powerful emotional response, such as fear or anger. Others are low key and linked to faint emotional responses, such as posed attention or calmness. Some learning environments are associated with learning difficulties and, therefore, evoke feelings of inadequacy, stress, or anxiety. Humans learn what is important to them at the moment. As a result, learners' emotional responses and cognitive development are interrelated.

> **REFLECTION** Imagine watching a movie whose audio is in an unfamiliar language. Do you rely on the English subtitles or stop periodically to translate unknown words? Ultimately, do you find the attention you expend on translation proves so taxing that it significantly interferes in your ability to follow the storyline and makes it difficult to persist for the entire movie? Do you feel frustrated? In what way is this situation analogous to Fatima's response in an English-only classroom?

How Language and Culture Shape Engagement

Learners are raised as members of a cultural group, and as cultural group members, they learn how to interact and use language. This process is called *language socialization* (Paradis et al., 2011). Learning language within a specific al environment actively shapes the affective networks and is the development of emotion, affect, and identity.

Interrelated language and cultural experiences impact engagement because they influence how learners' affective networks develop. In other words, language and culture shape how learners engage in the learning environment, such as who they engage with, when they speak, what they talk about, and even whether they prefer teacher-led to self-directed learning.

There are commonalities regarding how children are socialized within various cultures, but there are also stark differences. For example, North American parents (i.e., from Canadian and U.S.-dominant cultures) tend to treat their babies' vocalizations as meaningful attempts to communicate. Adults respond to infant babbling, burps, and smiling with verbalizations, playful interactions, and offers of food, toys, and physical comfort. Although Canadian Chinese parents also believe that infants' vocalizations are communication attempts, they are more likely to approach the exchange as an opportunity to teach language than to play. In contrast, Inuit mothers from Northern Canada tend not to interpret baby vocalizations as communication and may not respond verbally. Most often, Inuit children learn to speak primarily from siblings and other children. They are not expected to regularly converse with adults (Paradis et al., 2011). These different parent-to-child interactions impact how children develop language and influence the development of their affective networks, particularly in relation to how the children view the learning context. Children who initially learned language through play may find playful learning environments more engaging; children who learned language through direct adult-child instruction may feel more comfortable learning in direct instruction environments; and children who learned language from their siblings may avoid direct communication with teachers in the learning environment and be more engaged in learning peer-to-peer or in small groups.

Learning preferences is another way in which the development of the affective networks is reflected in how learners engage in the learning environment and can differ between cultures. For example, learners with a Navajo background may feel more comfortable in same-gender groups (Jordan, 1995). Studies also suggest that children from Hispanic backgrounds generally favor peer-to-peer collaborative work, and children from Cantonese families prefer teacher-directed lessons (Paradis et al., 2011). Teachers should be aware that when these learners are in a different learning environment than the one that they prefer, they may experience stress or anxiety. They may even refuse to join a group or follow the teacher's direction.

However, let's recall our discussion of learner variability in chapter 2. It's important *not* to ascribe generalizations as steadfast characteristics of all learners from specific cultural backgrounds. For instance, Sofia, a Hispanic learner, loathes collaborative work and Cheng, a Cantonese learner, relishes it. Nonetheless, teachers need to be aware that some learners from certain cultures may not feel comfortable in certain learning environments as a result of their cultural values and beliefs.

Context Is the Keystone

The keystone of an arch locks the structure together. Likewise, researchers studying the effects of affect believe that learning *context* is the keystone of learner success (Meyer, Rose, & Gordon, 2014). Figure 7.1 illustrates the crucial function of the keystone in an arch and how its role is analogous to the job of context in affective learning. Similar to the keystone stabilizing the arch, positive learning contexts secure learner engagement and achievement.

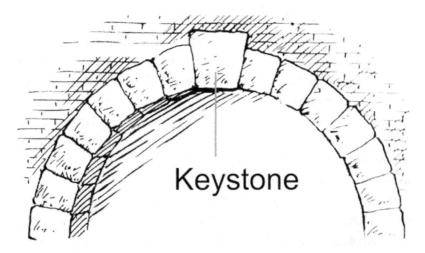

FIGURE 7.1: Context is the keystone. © ELI BROPHY, PHILADELPHIA, PA

Negative learning context or situations can cause stress or anxiety and lead to depressed student performance. For instance, studies show that minority students may perform more poorly in classrooms where they experience what is called *stereotype threat,* a phenomenon associated with stress over confirming negative stereotypes. In these classrooms, stigmatization and low expectations held by teachers and peers cause minority students to feel anxious, which in turn, results in lower performance (American Psychological Association, 2006). On the other hand, encouraging, self-affirming environments result in long-lasting positive learning effects.

---

*It's important **not to ascribe generalizations as** steadfast characteristics of all learners from specific cultural backgrounds.*

Multiple Means of Engagement

Designing a responsive learning environment begins with creating a safe, welcoming learning environment that engages all learners no matter what variability may exist. Note in figure 7.2 that in addition to recruiting interest and sustaining effort and attention, the UDL Guidelines under the UDL principle of Engagement also address self-regulation. Applying Culturally Responsive Design to instruction for ELs encourages educators to offer models and choices that are culturally and personally meaningful.

In addition, providing multiple means of engagement for CLD students includes setting and communicating expectations, and providing scaffolds, resources, and feedback to help learners to focus, persist, and succeed. To reduce frustration and anxiety, it's critically importance to offer challenges balanced by available resources. Table 7.1 suggests examples of UDL strategies that are effective for engaging CLD students and ELs.

Provide Multiple Means of

Engagement

Purposeful, motivated learners

Provide options for self-regulation
+ Promote expectations and beliefs that optimize motivation
+ Facilitate personal coping skills and strategies
+ Develop self-assessment and reflection

Provide options for sustaining effort and persistence
+ Heighten salience of goals and objectives
+ Vary demands and resources to optimize challenge
+ Foster collaboration and community
+ Increase mastery-oriented feedback

Provide options for recruiting interest
+ Optimize individual choice and autonomy
+ Optimize relevance, value, and authenticity
+ Minimize threats and distractions

FIGURE 7.2: UDL Guidelines for Engagement ©2014 CAST, INC. USED WITH PERMISSION

TABLE 7.1: Examples of effective strategies aligned with UDL Engagement Guidelines

UDL GUIDELINES FOR ENGAGEMENT	STRATEGY EXAMPLES
Provide options for recruiting interest • Optimize choice and autonomy • Optimize relevance, value, and authenticity • Minimize threats and distractions	• Create a welcome packet for newcomers • Teach survival language to newcomers • Assign a buddy to newcomers • Offer meaningful CRT models/choices • Confer with CLD students and ELs about their needs/goals • Connect learning goals to prior knowledge • Link learning goals to similar events/ideas in other cultures • Use semantic webbing to brainstorm content links to cultural backgrounds

UDL GUIDELINES FOR ENGAGEMENT	STRATEGY EXAMPLES
Provide options for sustaining effort and persistence • Heighten salience of goals/objectives • Vary demands and resources to optimize challenge • Foster collaboration and community • Increase mastery-oriented feedback	• Survey families re: goals • Share understandable versions of learning goals with students and parents • Offer resources responsive to demands • Offer opportunities to learn from peers • Pause periodically to allow learners time to catch up • Allow *think time* (5–7 seconds) after asking a question • Vary grouping; ELs work together and mixed groups of ELs with non-ELs • Emphasize positive interdependence of members of collaborative groups • Praise effort • Provide timely feedback on what is correct • Suggest *next steps* as corrective feedback • Rather than direct correction, restate incorrect statements using correct models
Provide options for self-regulation • Promote expectations and beliefs that optimize motivation • Facilitate personal coping skills and strategies • Develop self-assessment and reflection	• Maintain high expectations • Engage learners in designing expectations and rules • Teach coping strategies • Set specific, flexible learning goals • Teach learners to set personal learning goals • Teach learners to monitor and track their effort and progress • Provide correct L2 models • Selectively offer corrections to written and verbal L2 statements. • Offer opportunities to self-correct

Create a Welcoming Context

All learners need to feel safe and respected in order to learn and achieve. In particular, newcomers (i.e., recent immigrants) are likely to experience heightened levels of fear, anxiety, worry, and frustration even in the most positive classroom. It's important to offer them resources that provide a welcoming learning environment. Here are some suggested strategies:

- Create a welcome packet with visuals and translations of common vocabulary/phrases.

- Teach survival language, such as social greetings and asking for assistance.

- Post charts or pictures highlighting common directions and procedures.

- Assign a buddy, ideally a student who speaks the newcomers' L1.

- Get ELs a library card and show them where translated items are located.

Maintain High Expectations

Learners will aim for high expectations when they feel supported. Instead of lowering expectations for CLD students or developing separate academic goals just for them, offer a choice of production options. As discussed in chapter 3, maintaining high expectations is an important tenet of CRT. For example, if the learning goal is to identify and summarize the central ideas of a text (based on Common Core State Standard for English Language Arts, Reading Literature [CCSS ELA-LITERACY.RST 6-8.1) offer the option of completing a summary worksheet, creating an illustration, or sharing answers verbally with the teacher. Additional ideas include the following:

- Confer with CLD students and ELs and survey their families regarding educational goals.

- Link classroom learning expectations to similar events/ideas in L1 cultures and meaningful, culturally relevant objectives—i.e., how learning content is beneficial to the learner within her L1 environment.

- Share understandable or translated versions of learning goals with students and parents.

- Enhance learner self-assessment skills by brainstorming and designing expectations and rules as a class/group.

- Set specific, flexible learning goals (see chapter 8 for more about setting learning goals).

- Teach learners to set personal learning goals.

Balance Demands with Resources

In situations where students are unable to meet expectations, they can become anxious or frustrated. Although we've mentioned several times that maintaining high expectations is important, a balance must exist between expectations and instructional support. To be successful, learners need resources responsive to the demands of the learning environment. Link learning goals to learners' prior knowledge. Doing so will help learners make meaningful connections between previous lessons and new content. For example, at the beginning of each lesson, Aimee uses semantic webbing to brainstorm links between new content and what learners already know. This is also an excellent way to highlight connections with learners' cultural backgrounds. Other considerations for balancing demands with resources include the following:

- Pause periodically during presentations to allow learners time to translate and catch up.

- Allow *think time* (5–7 seconds) after asking a question to provide time for internal translation.

- Provide scaffolds that gradually release the responsibility or ownership of learning to learners over time (see more about scaffolds in chapter 6).

- Teach coping strategies, such as relaxation techniques and stop-and-think protocols, such as steps to use when students have difficulty, e.g., "First reread the instructions, then try it again, then ask a peer, then ask the teacher."

Employ Grouping as a Resource

Some cultures emphasize collaborative learning and the development of interdependence, sharing, and collaboration (Orosco & O'Connor, 2011). Others do not. (See chapter 3 for a discussion of collectivism vs. individualism.) In the learning environment, structured collaborative groups offer important opportunities to develop a sense of community. Cooperative learning tasks that require each group member to depend on the whole group's success are most effective. Be sure to vary grouping. When ELs who speak the same L1 work together, those with stronger L2 skills can provide translations and much-needed cultural explanations to those students who are still developing L2. In addition, ELs need to work in mixed groups with non-ELs who offer L2 language models and an opportunity to broaden peer relationships. In addition, keep these suggestions in mind:

- Promote positive interdependence by setting up groups of five or six to allow each student a role or specific task, e.g., one reads instructions, another sets up materials, a third keeps track of the time, a fourth records or illustrates their work, and a fifth reports results to the class.

- Teach cooperative listening skills, e.g., taking turns to listen and then providing feedback.

- Provide procedures for managing peer-to-peer and group conflicts, e.g., group members who ignore time allotments, refuse to complete assigned task, or disagree on goals or process.

- Use jigsaw tasks that rely on each learner completing a piece of the job.

Growth Mindset and Mastery Feedback

High expectations are linked to a growth mindset. As Carol Dweck (2016) states, learners with a fixed mindset avoid challenge, give up easily, and ignore feedback. They believe that effort is pointless. On the other hand, learners with a growth mindset embrace challenge, persist through setbacks, and learn from criticism. They believe that effort is part of mastery. Like the learner depicted in figure 7.3, a learner with a growth mindset is one who has an internal mantra of "not yet." Instead of thinking "I don't do well at math," the learner says, "I'm not yet where I want to be with math." A subtle but extremely important shift, "not yet" says "I can learn," and "I am going to learn."

FIGURE 7.3: Embracing a growth mindset © ELI BROPHY, PHILADELPHIA, PA

Educators who provide mastery-oriented feedback and praise effort promote the development of a growth mindset. Instead of giving nonspecific or vague feedback like, "You did a great job!", Dweck's (2016) research suggests that educators should comment on growth of an identified skill or area of knowledge. For example, if a student is working on the first draft of a writing project, offer feedback like, "I notice how you stuck with this draft and kept writing. That's a great way to improve your writing skills. I'm excited to see where this piece goes!" Feedback needs to be timely and focused on what's correct. To encourage improvements, teachers suggest *next steps* as part of their feedback. For instance, if your students are learning the technique of free writing, you might say, "I saw how you began by editing your work but that you shifted into free writing. That shows that you were willing to try the technique even if it was uncomfortable at first."

In each case, you draw the student's attention to a specific example or skill (e.g., completing a first draft or practicing free writing) and emphasize that you expect him to move forward with that specific ability. In addition, this type of feedback does not admonish the student for the times you had to push him to finish the first draft or for the times she scratched out words because she's a perfectionist. Your feedback moves them forward.

Mastery feedback can also help demystify the topic. For example, mathematics is viewed by some as a culturally neutral subject. However, Ukpokodu (2011) explains that the process of learning mathematics that is grounded in all cultures is based on universal human efforts to describe and understand the physical and social aspects of our experiences. As learners move through the academic processes of describing and understanding, it is imperative that they receive clearly articulated feedback, underscored by high expectations, to help them evaluate their progress during learning and discovery.

Let's recap: Remember that learning is emotional work. How learners respond in every learning environment is controlled by their affective networks which manage attention, persistence, and self-regulation (Meyer, Rose, & Gordon, 2014). Since all learners are raised as members of a cultural group, their cultural and linguistic experiences shape their affective networks. Educators can apply a variety of strategies to address the affective networks of culturally and linguistically diverse learners, including: (1) creating learning environments that are welcoming and safe, (2) maintaining high expectations, (3) balancing the demands of learning with appropriate, culturally relevant resources, (4) selectively focusing corrections of written and verbal L2 statements, and (5) offering varied grouping arrangements that develop stronger L2 skills and broaden peer relationships. In addition to providing mastery-oriented feedback to promote the development of a growth mindset, encourage learners to embrace challenge, persist through setbacks, and learn from criticism.

REFLECTION QUESTIONS

1. In what ways do CLD students and ELs experience unique challenges in terms of persistence and self-regulation?

2. What strategies can you use to address stereotype threat?

3. How does learning context make a difference?

4. To what extent will development of a learner's growth mindset improve self-regulation skills?

5. How can teachers engage culturally and linguistically diverse learners using the UDL Guidelines? What are viable options for recruiting interest, sustaining persistence, and self-regulation?

CHECK-IN: HOW DO YOU ENGAGE LEARNERS?

Using a 0–3 scale, how well do you integrate these UDL and CRT strategies into your learning environment?

CHECK-IN: HOW DO YOU ENGAGE LEARNERS?

1. Each day/class begins with a regular class routine.	O	1	2	3
2. New learning is connected to prior knowledge.	O	1	2	3
3. Learners help to determine the rules.	O	1	2	3
4. Learners know the rules because they are clear and consistent.	O	1	2	3
5. Learners' backgrounds contribute to class learning.	O	1	2	3
6. Learners have authentic, CRT options and choices.	O	1	2	3
7. All learners are held to high expectations.	O	1	2	3
8. Learners determine and monitor personal learning goals.	O	1	2	3
9. Learners have access to resources that match learning demands.	O	1	2	3
10. Mastery-oriented feedback encourages effort and achievement.	O	1	2	3

8

Culturally Responsive Lesson Design

This chapter follows a middle school team exploring how to use *Culturally Responsive Lesson Design*. Each of the team members infuses CRT strategies into a step of the UDL lesson planning process.

The Culturally Responsive Lesson Design process described in this chapter offers a guide for applying both CRT and UDL to lesson planning for ELs. It braids together ways to make sure that instruction is culturally responsive for all learners with UDL strategies that help you to address cultural and linguistic learner variability. The Culturally Responsive Lesson Design process is based on the step-by-step UDL lesson planning process described by Ralabate (2016), which consists of these six steps:

- Define flexible, clear, SMART learning goals

- Consider learner variability

- Determine appropriate assessments

- Select methods, materials, and media that add value

- Implement the lesson plan (teach)

- Refine educator learning through self-reflection

This chapter briefly summarizes each of the UDL lesson planning process steps and offers additional suggestions based on the CRT framework and exemplary second- or dual-language learning techniques. Culturally Responsive Lesson Design builds on and refines the UDL lesson planning process by emphasizing aspects of design important to effectively plan for CLD students and ELs.

Meet Leo and His Team

After the recent professional development workshop on UDL, Leo asks his seventh-grade team to consider infusing UDL into their revamped lesson design process. Always eager to learn, Tammy, an English teacher, agrees immediately. Jackie, however, expresses concern about losing new aspects of Culturally Responsive Teaching that the team uses to address the needs of their growing culturally and linguistically diverse population. Special education teacher Donovan wants to be sure that any new strategies would meet the needs of students with disabilities, particularly those who are also ELs. As a twenty-year veteran teacher, Christy is cautious about another big change. "Maybe we can do this in a step-by-step way so we don't become overwhelmed. We can build on the good things we're already doing," she suggests. As a team, they commit to a plan. Each team member will focus on infusing UDL with CRT into a separate step of their lesson design process and share their learning in their team meetings.

▶ In the Spotlight!

For detailed information about the UDL lesson planning process, see *Your UDL Lesson Planner: The Step-by-Step Guide to Teaching All Learners* (2016).

ONE STEP AT A TIME

Christy's concern about becoming overwhelmed is important to keep in mind. Transforming your practice takes time. In fact, sustainable changes in teacher beliefs and practices are the result of a continual process of growth (Guskey, 2000). Adopting an iterative process—selecting one area to change, moving forward, evaluating the impact of the change you've made, and then deciding whether to make another change—is a reasonable and effective way for individual educators, as well as teams and PLCs, to develop expertise.

Learning Goals: SMART, Flexible, Clear, and Responsive

Learning goals form the cornerstone for lessons and guide the selection of assessments, methods, materials, and media. All components of the lesson should align with its learning goals. In order for learners to understand what is expected of them, learning goals should be straightforward and coherently expressed in language that learners understand. Research shows that students make significantly more gains when teachers set clear learning goals (Marzano, Pickering, & Pollack, 2001). In this way, learning goals serve as a road map for both teachers and learners.

Make Learning Goals SMART

Many school districts across the United States encourage teachers to design learning goals that are SMART. A strategy borrowed from the business world, SMART goals are: Specific, Measurable, Attainable, Results-oriented, and Time-bound. Variations exist for the meaning of each letter in the acronym, but the bottom line is that learning goals need to be clearly defined, reasonable, and measured against accepted standards of learning.

Leo's team routinely writes SMART goals by considering the questions in table 8.1.

TABLE 8.1: SMART learning goals

SMART CHARACTERISTICS	SPECIFIC	MEASUREABLE	ATTAINABLE	RESULTS-ORIENTED	TIME-BOUND
Descriptions	Clearly state a specific student expectation	Provide timely evidence of learning derived from ongoing data or an appropriate assessment.	Include scaffolds within the learning statement to address barriers and readiness of all learners.	Focus on standards-based learner progress.	Define a specific time frame for accomplishing the goal.
Questions to ask	What do I want them to know or be able to do?	How am I going to know they learned it?	What assistance is needed for all learners to achieve the learning goal within a reasonable time frame?	How will learners move forward toward meaningful growth?	What is a reasonable endpoint for achieving this learning goal?
Examples	Learners will contrast points of view of three characters in Oliver Twist.	Learners will contrast points of view of three characters in Oliver Twist at a proficient level as measured by a descriptive rubric.	Given models and prompts as needed, learners will contrast points of view of three characters in Oliver Twist at a proficient level as measured by a descriptive rubric.	Given models and prompts as needed, learners will contrast points of view of three characters in Oliver Twist at a proficient level as measured by a descriptive rubric (based on CCSS RL 7.6: Analyze how an author develops and contrasts the points of view of different characters or narrators in a text).	By the end of the unit, given models and prompts as needed, learners will contrast the points of view of three characters in Oliver Twist at a proficient level as measured by a descriptive rubric (based on CCSS RL 7.6).

Design with Flexibility in Mind

Tammy, an English teacher, knows that effective learning goals are flexible. The UDL lesson planning process stresses using flexible verbs, rather than restrictive verbs, to allow learners multiple options for accomplishing the goal (Ralabate, 2016). For instance, the learning goal in table 8.1 is both specific and flexible. It requires students to contrast character points of view, but it does not stipulate exactly how they will express their understanding other than that their product will be evaluated by a rubric. Because the learning goal focuses on *contrasting* rather than a more restrictive action, such as writing, learners could write their analyses, or they could complete another task, such as developing a poster, completing a T-chart, or creating a comic. All learners have a choice. Designing the learning goal with a flexible verb (i.e., *contrast*), rather than a verb that limits their responses (i.e., *write*), offers learners many ways to achieve the goal. This approach is especially advantageous for ELs who may be struggling with speaking or writing in English.

Sometimes, the learning goal must contain a restrictive verb (such as write, read, or state) because the purpose of the lesson is to teach or develop a required skill. In this case, building in scaffolds can add needed flexibility and assist learners who may struggle with the required task. For instance, as an English teacher, Tammy ensures that her curriculum requires learners to develop their speaking, reading, and writing skills. Therefore, many of her learning goals contain restrictive verbs. She carefully embeds scaffolds, such as verbal models, oral prompts, and written cues, into her learning goals to offer support to learners who might need it. See chapter 6 for more detailed information about scaffolds.

Focus on Language Development

It's important to consider the language required during every lesson. Because almost all academic learning is language based, well-designed responsive lessons address mastery of *both* subject matter and language skills. One way to accomplish this is to develop separate learning goals. Thus, for each lesson, teachers design content-specific (i.e., academic knowledge and skills) learning goals based on subject matter standards and language-specific (i.e., listening, speaking, reading, and/or writing skills) goals based on language standards, such as the WIDA English Language Development (ELD) standards.

The UDL framework portrays the process of learning as a fluid and variable progression toward expert learning. Similarly, WIDA defines language development as a fluid, flexible, and ongoing process that is different for each student (WIDA, 2007). As discussed in chapter 5, WIDA's six ELD standards define second (L2) levels of proficiency in social, instructional, and academic language. They can be used as a basis for language-specific goals. WIDA Standards 2–5 specifically emphasize language required for academic success in the content areas of Language Arts, Mathematics, Science, and Social Studies (WIDA, 2014).

Maintain High Expectations

As described in chapter 2, expert teachers maintain high expectations for all learners without compromising or modifying learning goals. In other words, the cognitive demand for each lesson should be the same for all learners and across all levels of L2 development. The primary adjustments that teachers make are (1) adapting the language of instruction to support the comprehension levels of L2 learners, and (2) including scaffolds to address barriers that learners might encounter, especially CLD students and ELs. By exposing learners to rigorous academic vocabulary and content, well-defined learning goals challenge students while simultaneously allowing flexibility in how learners express their knowledge.

▶ **Bridge to CRT**

Chapter 3 discussed how important it is to uncover the dreams and goals of parents and families for their children. Teachers should share learning goals with families so that they can offer encouragement and support, as appropriate. For example, recognizing that collectivism is valued by the Japanese culture of many of Tammy's students' families, she highlights collaborative team effort in her learning goals. Also, because several parents are studying for their U.S. naturalization examination, she emphasizes the citizenship elements of her social studies curriculum in monthly school-to-home newsletters.

REFLECTION What's new for you about learning goals that align with UDL and CRT?

Variability: Core, Choice, and Challenge

Donovan, a special education teacher, felt that exploring the ways in which UDL and CRT address learner variability in lesson design were critically important. Keep in mind that the UDL Guidelines represent the systematic, predictable ways that learner variability is present in any group of learners, including CLD students and ELs. Previous chapters (i.e., 2, 3, 5) explain aspects of learner variability related to culture and L2 or dual-language learning. Every learner develops distinct patterns of learner variability based on the context of the learning environment and dynamic connections made during each experience. Fundamental to context, culture shapes experiences, and experiences shape learning. Learner variability is natural and expected.

Focus On the Core Cognitive Demand

Donovan realized that academic or content standards are broad statements that outline key expectations for what students should know or be able to do at specific stages during the school year. Also called learning standards, they are not the curriculum per se but they point to what teachers should teach. They usually take time to achieve, often more than one lesson. When you pare a standard to its core, you are able to identify its cognitive demand—the common task to expect of all students (WIDA, 2014). Focusing on the core cognitive demand as you write your learning goal allows you to build in choice and scaffolds while still holding all learners to the same expectations.

For example, the core cognitive demand for the learning goal in table 8.1 is to *contrast the points of view of different characters or narrators in a text* (based on Common Core State Standard for English Language Arts, Reading Literature 7.6, or CCSS RL 7.6). Therefore, the task for all learners is to contrast the points of view of different characters. All learners are held to the same expectation. What varies is how the students demonstrate their knowledge (i.e., choice) and how much assistance some learners will receive to achieve the goal (i.e., scaffolds).

Offer Choice and Challenge

For ELs, choice addresses learner variability across levels of English language proficiency. In other words, learning goals offer a choice in how learners demonstrate what they've learned. To address differences in L2 development, learning goals align linguistic demands with the learners' level of L2 proficiency. Chapter 5 described the six levels of language development according to WIDA (2014) (i.e., Level 1—Entering, Level 2—Emerging, Level 3—Developing, Level 4—Expanding, Level 5—Bridging, and Level 6—Reaching) and the five stages of language acquisition according to Hill and Miller (2013) (i.e., Silent/Receptive or Preproduction, Early Production, Speech

Emergence, Intermediate Language Fluency, and Advanced Language Proficiency). Both sets of developmental stages indicate potential linguistic abilities and demands that educators can use to build choice into their learning goals and lessons. Table 8.2 illustrates one way to align linguistic abilities with potential linguistic demands (i.e., listening, speaking, reading, writing) across six levels of L2 proficiency.

As described in chapter 7, be mindful to also offer challenge by systematically adjusting the demands slightly in response to the learner's performance. For example, as a special education teacher, Donovan uses gradual release of responsibility (GRR) to build linguistic skills over time (described in chapter 5). By continuing to vary and enhance demands, learning goals maintain interest, teach persistence, and optimize challenge for learners.

TABLE 8.2: Learner variability across L2 proficiency levels (based on WIDA, 2014)

LEVEL OF L2 PROFICIENCY	EXAMPLES OF LINGUISTIC DEMANDS
Level 1—Entering	**Nonverbal:** Act out scene, story, or pantomime response; use realia, blocks; draw picture, maps, graphs, charts; copy or use signs, gestures, point, body movements; sequence pictures to indicate narrative, timeline; create diorama
	Listen to short explanations with visual cues/ pictures; point to named pictures; respond to "Show me...; Find the..."
	Speak: Name/label pictures; use routine single-word responses; use greetings; participate in short choral speaking
	Read key or routine words; participate in short choral reading
	Write: Copy words from word bank; circle picture/ answer; complete cloze sentences by copying from text

LEVEL OF L2 PROFICIENCY	EXAMPLES OF LINGUISTIC DEMANDS
Level 2—Emerging	**Listen** to paragraphs, short stories with picture cues; listen for key words
	Speak: Answer yes/no; answer simple Wh-questions; name items, people, pictures; identify same/different
	Read academic vocabulary with visual cues; select word from list
	Write/copy simple sentences about pictures or visuals; make lists, brainstorm with scaffolds; group or categorize items; complete graphic organizers, charts, graphs that require short phrases or sentences
Level 3—Developing	**Listen:** Understand clear directions without visuals
	Speak in short phrases and sentences; engage in peer-to-peer conversations; participate in choral speaking; role-play
	Read flashcards; understand reading in context; locate key words within text; understand context cues
	Write: Match content vocabulary to descriptions; produce short sentences; complete poster/book cover/ bookmark, diorama; label map, chart, graph; complete sentence starters

LEVEL OF L2 PROFICIENCY	EXAMPLES OF LINGUISTIC DEMANDS
Level 4—Expanding	**Listen:** Understand descriptions, stories, core ideas without visuals; understand complex comprehension tasks with scaffolds; visualize based on description **Speak:** Describe creative ideas, analysis, hypothesis, steps in a process; debate, predict, draw conclusion independently; compare and contrast; respond to "why" and "how" questions; verbally respond to essay question **Read** and highlight or underline text; skim material for key information **Write** with grammatical and syntactical errors; use content vocabulary in writing; summarize, complete graphic organizers independently; use semantic webbing; write to prompt with assistance; self-edit; use translation dictionary
Level 5—Bridging	**Listen:** Comprehend at age/grade level without visuals **Speak** near age/grade level with visuals or scaffolds for complex vocabulary and sentence structure; respond to "what would happen if…" **Read** at or near age/grade level; use a study guide with assistance **Write** near age/grade level with writing guides and reminders for grammatical errors; write in journal
Level 6—Reaching	Listening, speaking, reading, and writing demands are comparable to age/grade-level expectations

> **REFLECTION** How are lessons focused on learner variability different from lessons you've developed before?

Assessment: Unbiased, Valid, and Informative

As a mathematics teacher, Christy believes that accurate assessment of learning is critically important. Assessment, the process of collecting information on student knowledge, skills, and dispositions, is more than simply giving one standardized test at the end of the year. Summative assessment, as the term implies, is used to measure comprehension and abilities at a specific point in time after learning is complete. It is an assessment *of* learning. Think of it as a snapshot—at the end of this unit, on this day, after this lesson, at this time of day, in this environment—a student was able to demonstrate that he understood this content or was able to do this task. Summative assessments include end-of-unit exams, mid-terms, final evaluations, final papers and projects, and most standardized tests (Ralabate, 2016; Rudner & Shafer, 2002).

On the other hand, formative assessment gathers information over time and focuses on the learning process and learner progress. It is an assessment *for* learning. As teachers and learners periodically check for improvement, they use this feedback to adjust their teaching and learning. Most classroom data collection is formative in nature and includes checks for understanding, student surveys, checklists, worksheets, and progress monitoring techniques (Ralabate, 2016; Rudner & Shafer, 2002).

Christy often uses formative assessments during her mathematics lessons. Formative assessments are flexible, meaningful, and matched to the learning goal. They measure whether your instruction is making a difference and whether learners are progressing along a continuum of learning targets (Ralabate, 2016). Both educators and students can use the meaningful classroom assessments to monitor progress. Formative classroom assessments are well suited for measuring progress; generally, standardized assessments are not.

Eliminate Bias

Christy realized that assessments need to be free of content or performance requirements that favor one subgroup of students over another. Referencing unique cultural experiences or unusual vocabulary that is only known to some learners benefits those test-takers and is an obstacle for others. For example, an exam that requires learners to describe the taste of bacon would disadvantage vegetarians and students who don't eat certain meats for religious reasons. Check illustrations, storylines, and perspectives for unwanted and hidden bias. Refrain from including cultural taboos and topics that could make learners uncomfortable. In addition, assessment items that characterize individuals by race, gender, ethnicity, religion, disability, socioeconomic, or other backgrounds are offensive and should always be avoided (Popham & Lindheim, 1980; Ralabate, 2016).

Check Validity

Any educator who is creating exams or analyzing ELs' standardized test results needs to be mindful of two aspects of assessment validity: (1) construct validity, and (2) the effect of translation on test validity. Construct validity refers to the degree to which an assessment tests what it says it tests (Rudner & Shafer, 2002). Research shows that including information that is unrelated to the main focus of the test (e.g., unnecessary linguistic complexity, cultural biases) affects the validity of high-stakes assessments for ELs (Abedi, 2010). How true is an assessment to its purported purpose? If a learner fails a third-grade mathematics exam that uses a sixth-grade lexicon level (i.e., vocabulary), did the student fail because he doesn't understand mathematics or because he doesn't know the language? Frankly, in this case the mathematics test score is not valid because the test doesn't measure what it is supposed to measure. The student's performance is more likely an indication of difficulty with language comprehension than mathematics skills.

In order for scores to be valid, standardized tests must be administered in a specific manner (i.e., using standard procedures). If a standardized assessment is given by an unqualified person or in a non-standardized manner (e.g., oral translation), the results are not valid and cannot be reported as a standard score. When local interpreters translate a standardized assessment, the scores cannot be reported because they are not valid.

Offer Accommodations

Every teacher is required at some point to provide accommodations for students with disabilities or ELs. It's important to understand some basics to ensure that you are providing exactly what your students need. Johnes (2006) defines accommodations as strategies, services, or supports provided to a student that do not change the content or level of expectations but can improve student engagement and increase the potential for success—for example, extended time, sign language interpreter, and large print. They are often described as assistance that levels the playing field by buffering barriers that suppress performance, such as limited L2. Different from accommodations, modifications change content or expectations and are rarely allowed during standardized tests. In the United States, states issue lists of approved accommodations for state standardized assessments that are administered to students with disabilities and ELs. If unapproved accommodations or modifications are used during a standardized assessment, the resulting scores are not valid. Learners should become familiar with test accommodations during classroom exams to ensure they can easily use them during a standardized assessment. Table 8.3 illustrates a variety of commonly used assessment accommodations.

TABLE 8.3: Common assessment accommodations aligned with UDL principles (based on Albus & Thurlow, 2007)

ENGAGEMENT	REPRESENTATION	ACTION AND EXPRESSION
Familiar Examiner/ Administration by Others The test is administered by someone the student knows rather than the regular test examiner, e.g., special education teacher, general education teacher, paraeducator.	*Large Print* Test is presented in large text.	*Proctor/Scribe/Pointing* Student responds verbally or by pointing and a proctor or scribe then translates this to an answer sheet.
Familiar Environment/ Small Group Administration The test is administered in a small or familiar room to control for distractions and lessen anxiety.	*Visual Cues* Provide visual prompts to focus attention (e.g., colored boxes around text) or highlight keywords (e.g., arrows, stickers) or as reminders (e.g., stop signs).	*Write in Test Booklet* Responses are written in the test booklet rather than on answer sheets, and school personnel then transcribe to answer sheets.

ENGAGEMENT	REPRESENTATION	ACTION AND EXPRESSION
Extended Time/ Frequent breaks The test is administered over a longer period of time or with opportunities for breaks to encourage persistence and lessen anxiety.	*Read Aloud* Directions or test items are read out loud.	*Computer/ Communication Device* Student responds using a computer or other device (e.g., typewriter, picture or symbol board, augmentative communication device).
	Repeat/Reread Clarify directions through restatement.	*Spell-checker/Grammar Check/Dictionary/ Bilingual Dictionary* Student uses spell checker or grammar checker either as a separate device or within a word processing program, or print materials (e.g., glossary, dictionary).
	Translate via L1 Directions and/or test items are translated.	*Tape Recorder* Student's verbal responses are tape recorded, generally for later transcription/ description.
	Sign Interpret Directions or test items/questions are presented via sign language, cued speech, signed English.	*Native Language Response* Student provides native language (L1) response.
	Additional examples Provided in response to student question.	*Brailler* Student uses a device or computer that generates responses in Braille.
	Braille Text is replaced by Braille symbols.	

Use Rubrics

Rubrics are scoring tools that can be used by teachers and students to assess both summative products and learning progress. Typically, they describe what is expected and what the learner must do to receive a certain score. They offer flexibility and choice, as well as an opportunity to develop student ownership and a growth mindset through mastery-oriented feedback. See Brookhart (2013) for an extensive discussion of how to develop effective rubrics.

> ▶ **Bridge to CRT**
>
> Christy was relieved to learn that infusing UDL into the assessment portions of her lesson design easily aligned with the CRT strategies she was already using. In particular, she realized that both UDL and CRT emphasize flexibility and student choice. She made sure that her assessments were unbiased and valid, and she provided accommodations to those students who needed them. Both EL and non-EL students benefited.

> **REFLECTION** How many barriers currently exist in the assessments that you use in your classroom? What strategies could you use to help learners overcome those barriers?

Contextualize Methods, Materials, and Media

Jackie, a science teacher, wanted to learn more about both CRT with UDL. She was particularly concerned with learning ways that she could build content knowledge and strengthen her students' Cognitive Academic Language Proficiency (i.e., academic vocabulary skills of her ELs).

Build Content Knowledge with Sheltered English Instruction

Structured English Instruction, also called Sheltered English Immersion (SEI), is an approach for teaching ELs that focuses on encouraging English proficiency through language-rich, grade-level content instruction (Markos & Himmel, 2016). When paired with bilingual content instruction (if available), ELs are able to progress academically at the same time that they are learning English. As students' English proficiency advances, their exposure to and participation in English-based content instruction increases. The most common SEI model is the Sheltered Instruction Observation Protocol (SIOP) model developed for Pearson by Echevarria, Vogt, and Short (2017). Features of SEI include the following:

- Focusing on content and language goals

- Connecting content with learners' backgrounds

- Teaching content vocabulary and academic language

- Using context-embedded strategies and materials

- Using cooperative learning to promote language development

- Using assessments that can measure content knowledge regardless of English proficiency

A key aspect in SEI is that subject matter teachers explicitly teach second-language acquisition as well as content. For instance, Jackie learned that she should not only consider the science standards for her science lesson planning but that she should also deconstruct what key words, concepts, and academic vocabulary are needed in order to successfully achieve each science learning objective. She could then explicitly teach the content-specific words as part of her lesson. In another example, Riley not only wants her math students to understand how to use different computational methods, but she also wants them to understand words specific to mathematics. She incorporates various vocabulary strategies in her math lessons to teach (1) common English words related to mathematics (e.g., more, less), (2) synonyms or different vocabulary that are used to refer to math operations (e.g., subtract, take away, deduct, minus, debit), and (3) language that helps learners interpret math problems (e.g., problem, solution, reasoning).

Provide Scaffolds

Typically, SEI lessons provide opportunities for ELs to develop the four domains of language: listening, speaking, reading, and writing. Since these skills are still developing, ELs will likely need scaffolds to address learner variability and enhance learning. Scaffolds should directly remove barriers related to L2 linguistic development during the lesson. See chapter 6 for descriptions of scaffolds and how to use them.

Select Culturally Responsive Materials and Media

Classroom instructional materials should incorporate multicultural information and resources. Textbooks and literature should reflect students' ethnic, linguistic, and cultural perspectives and classroom displays should represent different cultures. To create a more welcoming environment, label classroom objects with multilingual tags. In addition, educators need to analyze textbooks, materials, and media for bias. Any materials that denigrate subcultures should be eliminated unless the lesson focuses specifically on social justice issues. If possible, work with school and public librarians or media specialists to ensure a variety of bilingual resources is available.

▶ Bridge to CRT

A science teacher, Jackie realized that she did not have to use a different curriculum or adopt mannerisms associated with students' cultural communities to apply CRT methods. Doing this would not be authentic and may even be insulting to culturally and linguistically diverse learners. Instead, offering culturally meaningful choices and opportunities for students to share their culture with the rest of the class is a far more successful approach.

Jackie found a natural blend between UDL and CRT. Teachers can actively connect academic content to students' everyday experiences to recruit interest and maintain engagement during lessons. Remember (from chapter 7) the importance of context to learning: context is the keystone for building deep understanding. To link school with home and the community, teachers can begin lessons by asking about learners' prior knowledge. This recognizes cultural influences and contextualizes learning. They can also look for ways to integrate student cultures into the classroom by carefully selecting culturally appropriate materials and media, such as multicultural books, native scenarios and legends, and video stories. Finally, inviting family members and community leaders to the classroom allows them to share how their work relates to academic content.

Refine Culturally Responsive Design Through Reflection

The final, critically important step in the Culturally Responsive Design process is reflection. Every teacher can apply purposeful reflection to improve her instructional practice. To engage in effective, results-oriented reflection, you need to review student work, performance, data, or quantifiable evidence of learning. Examining student data serves two purposes: (1) you can evaluate and grade learner performance, and (2) you can determine the effectiveness of your lesson planning process (Ralabate, 2016).

Target Expert Learning and Teaching

The purpose of applying UDL and CRT to instruction is to support expert learning among all students, including CLD students and ELs. As you will recall from chapter 1, expert learners are resourceful, knowledgeable, and strategic in their learning (Meyer, Rose, & Gordon, 2014). Expert learners are motivated to learn and purposefully use self-reflection as they monitor achievement of their goals.

As we discussed in chapter 1, Hattie (2003) describes expert teachers as educators who "engage students in learning and develop in their students' self-regulation, involvement in mastery learning, enhanced self-efficacy, and self-esteem as learners" (p. 9). Applying a UDL lens, another description of expert teachers is that they (1) know how to apply effective instructional strategies to address learner variability and develop learners' self-regulation skills, (2) possess a deep understanding of their own strengths and needs as a teacher, and (3) are committed to continuous improvement and a growth mindset.

By combining planning and reflection aspects of UDL and CRT, expert teachers maintain a razor-sharp focus on developing expert learners. Essentially, the Culturally Responsive Design process guides them to accomplish the following:

- Define SMART, flexible learning goals that hold all learners to high expectations.

- Develop lessons that are responsive to cultural and linguistic variability.

- Ensure fair, unbiased assessments.

- Develop culturally relevant lessons that enhance both language acquisition and academic achievement.

- Select methods, materials, and media that add value.

▶ Bridge to CRT

Each teacher on Leo's team was an expert learner. As the team leader and a social studies teacher, Leo decided to investigate how UDL and CRT could add to the team's reflection process. He felt that UDL's emphasis on flexibility and choice aligned well with the culturally responsive strategies that the team was already using. In addition, he believed that applying a Culturally Responsive Design approach to their instruction would help them to improve their practice as expert teachers. Using the UDL principles, the CRT framework, and Bloom's taxonomy as guides, Leo and his team designed reflection questions they could apply to their lesson reflection process:

1. What did we do to engage CLDs and ELs, to represent information, and to offer choice of expression?

2. Did all learners meet the learning goal(s)? If not, why not?

3. What had the greatest impact on learner success?

4. To what extent can we replicate the strengths of this lesson?

5. How does this lesson compare with other lessons?

6. What didn't work? How can it be improved?

7. What's next? How will we continue to grow?

In summary, Culturally Responsive Lesson Design guides teachers in developing culturally relevant lessons that enhance both language acquisition and academic achievement. Focused on the core cognitive demand, lessons are rigorous and challenging while simultaneously offering flexibility in how learners express their learning. Leo and his team found that all subject matter teachers should explicitly teach second-language acquisition as well as content. In addition, they should leverage context and culture, and select culturally responsive materials and media. What does this mean for you? Ultimately, applying Culturally Responsive Design will help you enhance your practice as you become an expert at culturally responsive UDL design for all learners.

REFLECTION QUESTIONS

1. How does articulating clear, flexible goals help educators choose options (in assessment, methods and materials) that maintain high expectations for learners, especially ELs?

2. To what extent will learner variability and the language learning needs of ELs change your lesson planning process?

3. In what ways can UDL-aligned assessment techniques effectively address barriers that impact the performance of ELs?

4. How can the UDL Guidelines help you analyze how different kinds of materials/media/tools can provide scaffolds for ELs?

CHECK-IN: REFLECTION WORKSHEET FOR RESPONSIVE LESSON DESIGN

Review a recent or favorite lesson that is fresh in your mind. Complete the Reflection Worksheet for Responsive Lesson Design. Share your responses with a colleague.

REFLECTION QUESTION	YOUR RESPONSE
1. What did I do to engage CLD students and ELs, to represent information and to offer choice of expression?	
2. Did all learners meet the learning goal(s)? What had the greatest impact on their success?	
3. To what extent can I replicate the strengths of this lesson?	
4. How does this lesson compare with other lessons?	
5. What didn't work? How can it be improved?	
6. What's next? How will I continue to grow?	

The Policy Foundation

To truly appreciate the significance of CRT and how UDL can benefit ELs and CDL students, teachers need to understand how students' civil rights lay a foundation for making instructional decisions. This chapter offers a brief review of U.S. federal policy relevant to bilingual education, special education, and UDL. For the purposes of this discussion, policy refers to federal legislation, state laws, court rulings, administrative regulations, and national policy reports. What follows for some of you might seem like a review of your high school civics class or college special-education law course. For others, you might glean critical new information that can protect learners from being misidentified or denied needed services.

● Meet Lee

As the diversity in her school increases and many more students struggle with her course content, Lee is contemplating whether to refer students who are falling behind to the school early intervening team. In particular, Chin seems totally lost during Algebra class and never hands in any work. He's been in the United States for at least two years. "Shouldn't he be doing better?" she wonders.

The school counselor tells her that students who are receiving ESL services can't receive special education services, so they shouldn't be referred until they've failed for three years. Other teaching colleagues blatantly ignore this rule and flood the response to intervention (RTI) team with EL referrals as early as October. "Is Chin even eligible for special education services?" Lee wonders. She wants to do what's best for Chin and her other struggling EL students, but she doesn't know if they have the same rights as other students.

Unfortunately, Lee's dilemma is not that unusual. Teachers can be uninformed and misinformed about their students' rights. As a result, some students who have disabilities never receive the special education services they need and other students are inappropriately identified as disabled when what they really require is additional language support and time to develop academic language skills. Knowledge is power. Not only do well-informed educators design suitable instruction to meet individual learner needs, but they also advocate on behalf of their students to ensure that they receive appropriate programming and services. Read on to discover what civil rights ELs have and what laws, court cases, and policy statements laid the groundwork for applying UDL to instruction. As you read, note that key rights granted by federal policies are highlighted in italics.

EVOLUTION OF A TAPESTRY OF POLICIES

It might surprise you to hear that almost everything you do as a teacher was at one time addressed in federal or state policy. Over the last 240 years, a tapestry of policies interwoven with landmark bilingual and special education laws and civil rights court cases evolved into the rules that govern public education in the United States. To develop a full understanding of how they impact the education of ELs, it's worthwhile to start at the beginning.

U.S. Constitution—The Cornerstone

The cornerstone for bilingual and special education is the principle of *equal opportunity*, which can be traced back to the Declaration of Independence and the U.S. Constitution. Specifically, the 14th Amendment of the U.S. Constitution ensures equal protection under the law to all citizens (Baca & Cervantes, 2004).

Many national leaders refer to education as a national priority. However, unlike numerous other countries, the United States does not technically have a federal system of education. The 10th Amendment of the U.S. Constitution requires a separation of federal from state powers by stipulating that all powers not specifically granted to the federal government become the responsibility of the states (Osborne & Russo, 2014). Education is one of those responsibilities. It is the responsibility of the states, not the federal government, to provide public education. If you are a public school employee, you may know of state education codes or state education regulations that impact what or how you teach. In fact, states often bristle in response to prescriptive federal education mandates from Congress, calling them an encroachment on *states' rights*.

Historically, funding was the primary role of the federal government, to assist states in offering appropriate education and to incentivize reforms at state and local levels. Most national education laws authorize federal funding that supplements state and local funding. For example, federal special education funding doesn't cover the complete cost of special education services offered at the local level. It is designed to encourage states to offer special education programs aligned with federal law, but it does not supplant regular state and local education funding. States can refuse to accept federal monies at any time and the federal government can withhold federal special education funding if states violate the law. However, this rarely happens. In reality, federal monies account for less than 8–10 percent of the total cost of public education with the bulk of education funding coming from state and local taxes (U.S. Department of Education, 2007).

Since the states are responsible for public education, they set up their own structures, including entrance and graduation requirements, curriculum, assessment systems, teacher certification guidelines, and funding mechanisms to provide monies to local school districts. Hence, each state's education system is independent and different. Yet they tend to share ideas and readily copy initiatives from one another.

Generations of Neglect and Segregation

Unfortunately, it took generations before the rights bestowed by the U.S. Constitution directly impacted the education of ELs and students with disabilities. As Americans became more enlightened about individual abilities and differences, community biases and perspectives changed over time and were reflected in the courts.

Evolving Perspectives

Baca and Cervantes (2004) describe the following five periods of federal perspectives toward educating students who have special needs, including ELs:

- *Period of Neglect* (1776–1817). In the early years of our country, formal education was reserved for the wealthy and privileged. Students without economic means, and those needing special instruction, were totally left out of educational offerings. Not only were their educational needs neglected, but they were often physically secluded as far away from other people as possible.

- *Age of Asylums* (1817–1869). As the availability of public education increased, there was growing recognition that students with special needs should be taken care of. A sense of pity caused parents and communities to set up separate, large institutions to house individuals who were different in some way. Expectations were extremely low and students were not provided with instruction as we know it today.

- *Period of Separate Day Schools* (1869–1913). During this period, there was a growing understanding that some students could learn if provided with certain types of instruction. States established residential special schools, separate programs, and day classes for students with specific needs, such as deafness, blindness, or physical disabilities.

- *Period of Public School Programs* (1913–1950). The trauma and aftermath of two global wars caused an uptick in state compulsory education laws and child labor restrictions as policy makers became more cognizant of the educational needs of the "common" people. Across the country, there was an explosion of neighborhood public schools. However, students who struggled academically or had special needs continued to be relegated to segregated or separate classes within public school buildings or excluded from public education entirely.

- *Age of Equity* (1950–present). Over the last sixty-five years, federal policies and cultural changes have emerged that acknowledge the civil rights of individuals with disabilities and ELs. Incrementally, public schools have assumed their responsibility to establish opportunities for students with special needs to be educated alongside non-EL and non-disabled peers.

As the scales of justice depicted in figure 9.1 imply, we are living in the Age of Equity. Many of the issues you face every day in your classroom—how to meet the needs of culturally diverse students, how to provide an inclusive learning environment for students with disabilities, or how to ensure that struggling learners are able to pass state-mandated assessments—are the result of centuries of societal changes.

FIGURE 9.1: Scales of justice © ELI BROPHY, PHILADELPHIA, PA

Reflective Courts

The U.S. judicial system is often a reflection of prevailing public attitudes and opinions rather than a strict adherence to literal statutory language. As a result, the courts were not always as enlightened and protective of students with special needs as they might be today. In fact, some of the earliest court decisions may be quite shocking to you. The following cases from early U.S. history illustrate that prior to the 1960s, students with special needs were not permitted an equal opportunity or even the right to access a public education.

- *Watson v. City of Cambridge* (1893). A Massachusetts Supreme Judicial Court ruled that a child "weak in mind" could not benefit from instruction, was troublesome to other children, was unable to take "ordinary, decent, physical care of himself," and therefore could be expelled.

- *Beattie v. Board of Education* (1919). A Wisconsin court ruled that a student who drooled, had facial contortions, and experienced speech problems could be excluded because his condition "nauseated" teachers and other students, required too much teacher time, and negatively affected school discipline and progress.

- *Department of Public Welfare v. Haas* (1958). An Illinois Supreme Court ruled that the state's compulsory attendance law did not require the state to provide a free public education for "feeble-minded" or "mentally deficient" children who, because of their limited intelligence, were unable to reap the benefits of education.

> **REFLECTION** Imagine if any of these rulings were voiced as a decision today. What do you think would be the reaction of your school's parent group or community representatives? The teaching staff? Your students?

Civil Rights Gains Transformed Education

Since 1954, significant civil rights gains for students with special needs have transformed public education in the U.S. (Osborne & Russo, 2014). In fact, more has been done over the last six decades to open up educational opportunities available to all students than the previous two centuries. In some ways, these policy changes have had a snowball effect. Once a benefit was offered to one group of students, it set a precedent that advocates used to achieve the same benefit for other groups of students.

As federal bilingual and special education policies emerged, certain student rights were guaranteed: (1) equal education opportunity, (2) free appropriate public education (FAPE), (3) procedural safeguards/due process, (4) nondiscriminatory practices, particularly in evaluations, (5) least restrictive environment (LRE)/mainstreaming/inclusion, (6) continuum of bilingual programs and special education services, and (7) parent participation. In addition, key concepts appeared in federal legislation and court judgments: (1) ability to benefit from education, (2) categories/classification systems, (3) specially designed instruction and individualized education programs (IEPs), and (4) reasonable accommodations. Do any of these sound familiar to you? Look for these rights and concepts highlighted in italics in the brief court case and statutory descriptions listed here:

- *Brown v. Board of Education (BOE) of Topeka, Kansas* (1954). Most educators know about this court case. Focused on the education of African American students, this U.S. Supreme Court decision stated that each child has a right to the *equal opportunity of a public education* and that substituting access to *a separate education is unconstitutional*. This precedent-setting guarantee of equal protection was based on the 14th Amendment of the U.S. Constitution (i.e., the equal protection clause).

- *Title VI of the Civil Rights Act of 1964.* In response to calls for equal opportunity and nondiscrimination from civil rights activists, Congress passed the Civil Rights Act in 1964. Title VI of the Act *prohibits discrimination* based on race, color, or national origin in programs or activities that receive federal funding. Most of us realize that this law impacts voting rights, but were you aware that it applies to all public entities, including public schools?

- *Elementary and Secondary Education Act (ESEA)* (1965). Passed as part of President Lyndon Johnson's War on Poverty and in direct response to a demand for *equal education opportunity* for children living in low-income neighborhoods, the Elementary and Secondary Education Act (ESEA) was the first effort of the federal government to offer guidance on how states should be providing public education. It offered federal funding to local districts that set up remedial programs for children and schools impacted by poverty and is still influencing schools today.

- *Amendments to the ESEA, Title VI - PL 89-750* (1966). In 1966, Congress passed amendments to ESEA that included the first federal assistance to provide *appropriate education for children with disabilities*, through a targeted grant program. It provided funds to local schools rather than state-operated schools or institutions. It also established the federal Bureau of Education for the Handicapped (BEH) to administer programs for children with disabilities (now known as the Office of Special Education Programs) and the National Advisory Council (now known as the National Council on Disability).

- *Bilingual Education Act – PL 90-247* (1968). As part of amendments to ESEA in 1968, Congress passed the first federal legislation focused on bilingual education as a competitive grant program for local schools. These programs later become known as discretionary grant programs. Through federal funding, schools were encouraged to voluntarily establish *bilingual programs* designed to meet the needs of students with limited English proficiency (LEP) (now referred to as English learners).

- *Handicapped Children's Early Education Assistance Act – PL 90-538* (1968). This Act was the first federal statute focused solely on children with disabilities. It established funding for 75–100 model programs across the country for preschool children with disabilities. It included provisions for *parent participation*, community relationships, and authorized federal appropriations.

- *Education of the Handicapped Act – PL 91- 230* (1970). Congress passed amendments to ESEA that consolidated a number of separate federal grant programs into Title VI, known as the Education of the Handicapped Act. It established model *programs for children with learning disabilities* funded through grants to states; special grants for research and training programs, including higher education grants to train special education teachers; and regional resource centers.

Figure 9.2 illustrates a comprehensive list of students' rights defined through the above judicial and legislative actions and those that followed in the 1970s.

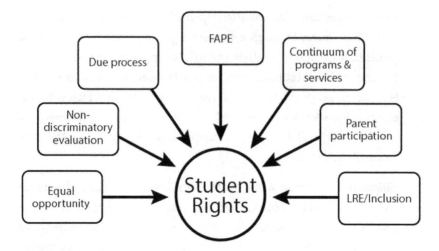

FIGURE 9.2: Guaranteed student rights ©ELI BROPHY, PHILADELPHIA, PA

Social Justice: A Springboard for Disability and Education Rights

Advocates used increasing national awareness of civil rights issues sur-
facing as a result of the civil rights and the women's rights movements
as a springboard for acquiring rights for the disabled and ELs (Baca &
Cervantes, 2004). Several court cases were precursors to today's
special and bilingual education policy. See how many you recognize.

- *Pennsylvania Association for Retarded Children (PARC) v. PA*
  (1971). This court case focused on students with mental retardation as a group. In this case, the court held that (1) all children are
  capable of *benefiting from an education,* (2) students with mental
  retardation had the right to a free appropriate public education
  (FAPE), and (3) denying students with disabilities access to a free
  public education was a violation of the Constitution's 14th Amendment because they were not being provided with "equal protection under the law."

- *Mills v. BOE of the District of Columbia* (1972). This court case
  focused on students with disabilities as a group. Based on the 14th

Amendment, this decision stated that students with disabilities were being excluded from public education without due process. It established the constitutional right of children with disabilities to a public education "commensurate with their ability to learn." The court linked its decision to the *Brown v. Board of Education* decision by noting that *separating or excluding students was unconstitutional.* The court ordered due process safeguards that addressed *labeling/classifying* students as disabled and how to determine educational placements for students with disabilities. The court's decision stipulated these *due process rights*:

- Right to a hearing with representation, a record, and an impartial hearing officer

- Right to appeal

- Right to have access to records

- Right to receive a written parental notice at each stage of the due process procedures.

- *Aspira of NY v. BOE of New York City* (1972). This court case focused on bilingual students as a group. Aspira, a group that advocated on behalf of bilingual students, filed suit against the New York City Board of Education, claiming that their education opportunities were being denied because these students did not speak English. It resulted in a consent agreement (called the Aspira Decree) that secured the *right of bilingual students to a bilingual education.*

- *Lau v. Nichols* (1974). Focused on Chinese students in California, this court case was one of the most significant cases to impact ELs. This U.S. Supreme Court decision ruled that equal treatment does not lead automatically to equal opportunity. In other words, equal treatment is not always fair. Bilingual educators view this decision as discerning the issue of "equity" for bilingual students by focusing on "equality of outcomes," rather than a one-size-fits-all approach to programs.

- *Dyrcia S. et al. v. BOE of New York* (1979). This court case focused on Puerto Rican and other Hispanic LEP students with disabilities as a group. The court found that these students were not being provided with an appropriate education and called for bilingual special education programs by doing the following:

  - Establishing school-based support teams to evaluate students with a bilingual, *nondiscriminatory evaluation process*

  - Setting up appropriate programs in the *least restrictive environment*

  - Offering a *continuum of bilingual special education services*

  - Requiring Spanish versions of *due process* and parental rights information

  - Providing *parental involvement* programs

- *Larry P. v. Wilson Riles* (1979). This court case addressed Black children in California public schools as a group. The court ruled that IQ testing of racial minorities was discriminatory when used for placement decisions into special education programs and called for *nondiscriminatory evaluation* methods.

> **REFLECTION** How do you think desegregation efforts for ethnic and racial minorities opened up access to public school for students with disabilities? To what extent do you see connections between these two issues?

1970s: Congress Takes Action

You may have heard that the 1970s were a time of civil and social unrest in the United States. During the 1970s, Congress thrust itself into the social justice and educational opportunity arena by enacting a long list of federal legislation related to civil rights and bilingual or special education. Interestingly, the federal government was concerned about bilingual education before it became involved with education for students with disabilities. For example, Congress passed the Bilingual Act in 1968—five years prior to the passage of the first law that addressed disability rights (the Rehabilitation Act of 1973), and seven years prior to the first federal special education law (the Education of All Handicapped Children Act of 1975).

- *Section 504 of the Rehabilitation Act* (PL 93-112) (1973). Many educators are familiar with 504 plans. They actually derive from this law, the first civil rights statute primarily focused on providing job opportunities and training to adults with disabilities. A single paragraph, which is now referred to as Section 504, stated that individuals with disabilities could no longer be excluded or denied participation in a program or activity that was supported by federal funds. Since they receive federal funding, public schools are required to provide these same protections. According to Section 504, individuals with disabilities that substantially affect a major life function (such as learning) must be provided with *reasonable accommodations* or modifications, and an *equal opportunity* to succeed. To clarify, the focus of Section 504 is not education but *nondiscrimination*, and 504 plans focus on providing accommodations, not special education.

- *Education for All Handicapped Children Act* (PL 94-142) (1975). In 1975, the first federal statute requiring states and local schools to educate students with disabilities was passed by Congress and signed by President Gerald Ford. It went into effect in October 1977 when the regulations were finalized. In 1990, its name changed during its reauthorization to the Individuals with Disabilities Education Act (IDEA). The original Act addressed the following:

    - Establishing a right to a free, appropriate public education (FAPE)

    - Protecting the rights of students and their parents/families in securing FAPE through *procedural safeguards*

- Assisting state and local education agencies (schools and districts) to provide for the education of students with disabilities by authorizing federal funding

- Assessing and assuring the effectiveness of state and local efforts to educate students with disabilities

- Establishing the right to placement in the *least restrictive environment* (LRE), which was originally referred to as *mainstreaming* and is now referred to as *inclusion*.

- Defining *individualized education programs* (IEPs) for students with disabilities who qualified for special education services

Federal Protections and Expectations Increase

Court rulings and federal legislation through the 1980s and 1990s defined and clarified the rights of students and their parents under special and bilingual education laws. In addition, expectations for students with disabilities and ELs steadily increased in the twenty-first century to a level comparable to all other students.

- *Handicapped Children's Protection Act* (PL 99-372) (1986). Congress amended the Education of the Handicapped Act of 1970 to authorize the award of reasonable attorney's fees to parents who prevail in due process hearings/court cases.

- *Education of the Handicapped Amendments* (PL 99-457) (1986). This legislation reauthorized and amended the Education of All Handicapped Children Act by lowering the eligibility for special education and related services to age three. The amendments also created the Handicapped Infants and Toddlers Program (Part H) by establishing federal funding incentives to educate children from birth to their third birthday (Birth-3) using early intervention strategies defined in *individualized family service plans* (IFSPs).

- *Individuals with Disabilities Education Act* (PL 101-476) (1990). During this reauthorization of the Education of All Handicapped Children Act, the name of the law was changed. Other changes included the following:

  - Adding traumatic brain injury (TBI) and autism as disability categories

  - Requiring that IEPs address transition services

  - Adding assistive technology services as a special education service

  - Including rehabilitation counseling and social work services as related services

- *Americans with Disabilities Act* (1990). The ADA applied *discrimination protection based on disability to all individuals, including adults* in all public and private sites, including the workplace and in postsecondary environments. It was the first time that private entities, including private schools, were required to provide equal access to individuals with disabilities.

- *Individuals with Disabilities Education Act Amendments* (PL 105-17) (1997). Congress reauthorized the Individuals with Disabilities Education Act (IDEA '97) and added significant changes:

  - Added a regular education teacher to IEP team

  - Added attention deficit disorder (ADD) and attention deficit hyperactivity disorder (ADHD) as conditions that could qualify a student for special education services under the category of Other Health Impaired (OHI)

  - Clarified disciplinary provisions to allow students with disabilities to be excluded from school for up to 10 cumulative days for disciplinary action such as suspension without it being considered a change of placement that required a review by the IEP team

- Required states to offer mediation to parents/families prior to due process hearings

- Required IEP teams to define the inclusive environment for each student by describing in the student's IEP how he or she was to be involved in the general education curriculum.

- *No Child Left Behind* (PL 107-110) (2002). You've probably heard of this one and you may have experience with its implementation. In a bipartisan partnership, Congress reauthorized ESEA as the No Child Left Behind Act (NCLB) and incorporated most of President George W. Bush's priorities into the new law. Title I required schools to include all students with disabilities and ELs in state standardized assessments and held schools and districts accountable for ensuring that all students, including students with disabilities and ELs, were able to meet grade-level proficiency by the 2013–2014 school year. Schools, districts, and states were required to make adequate yearly progress (AYP) to avoid sanctions, such as takeovers and school closures. Title III, titled "Moving limited English proficient students to English fluency," required schools to emphasize English proficiency for ELs. ESEA/NCLB had four purposes:

  - *Increase accountability for student performance,* holding schools and states accountable for their effectiveness by annual state reading and math assessments in grades 3–8.

  - *Focus on what works* by targeting federal resources to programs that were research based, enhancing teacher quality by establishing a federal definition for "highly qualified teachers," and requiring that all teachers meet this definition by 2005–06.

  - *Reduce bureaucracy and increase flexibility* by providing additional funding and flexibility to local schools to produce results. If schools did not meet performance goals, they could lose funding.

  - *Empower parents* to leave under-performing schools through a public school choice program.

- *Individuals with Disabilities Education Improvement Act* (PL 108-446) (2004). IDEA 2004 was a substantial revision of the federal special education law. It aligned assessment requirements for students with disabilities with the assessment and accountability provisions of NCLB, included a definition for a highly qualified special education teacher based on NCLB's definition, removed the requirement for short-term objectives in IEPs except for students with severe cognitive disabilities, prohibited states from requiring a discrepancy IQ model to identify students as learning disabled (LD), and encouraged states to use a response to intervention (RtI/RTI) approach prior to qualifying students for special education services under the LD category.

- *Every Student Succeeds Act (ESSA)* (2015). This reauthorization of ESEA/NCLB eliminated many of the more onerous components of NCLB. For example, the authority for school accountability was transferred from the federal government back to the states and local districts. Although the requirement was maintained for annual statewide assessments in grades 3 through 8, and once in high school for reading and math, and three times between grades 3 and 12 in science, the adequate yearly progress (AYP) provisions were repealed. The definition of a highly qualified teacher was also removed. Students with disabilities and ELs continue to be included in statewide assessments with access to accommodations, as appropriate, and accountability systems.

Federal Recognition for Universal Design for Learning

As you may have noted, most of the federal legislation listed in this chapter addresses rights for students and requirements for educators, schools, and states. There is little mention of instructional strategies or approaches. From the beginning of the twenty-first century, national policies and federal legislation focused on providing equal education opportunities (FAPE) through inclusion in general education curriculum. To that end, and in an uncharacteristic move, Universal Design for Learning (UDL) was officially defined in legislation and identified as an effective approach.

- *Higher Education Opportunity Act* (2008). When the Higher Education Act of 1965 was reauthorized in 2008, UDL was included as a means of reducing barriers by building appropriate supports and challenges into instruction. This Act included the first federal definition of UDL. The law also emphasized that all teacher candidates should receive instruction in strategies that are consistent with UDL in their preservice training. You may have participated in professional learning focused on UDL as a direct result of this Act.

- *National Education Technology Plan* (2010). This report was released by the U.S. Department of Education as a guide for the use of information and communication technologies. UDL was defined in the report as a framework for reducing barriers and maximizing learning opportunities for all students. UDL was referred to throughout the plan as a way to ensure that technology is used to optimize learning for all learners.

- *Common Core State Standards (CCSS)* (2010). The CCSS was a state-led effort to establish shared standards as the purpose for instruction to ensure that all students are career and college ready. UDL was highlighted as a means of applying CCSS to instruction for students with disabilities and ELs. Although some states have moved away from their initial focus on the CCSS, standards-based instruction continues to be prevalent throughout the country.

- *Every Student Succeeds Act (ESSA)* (2015). The newest reauthorization of ESEA, the *ESSA* includes a definition of UDL as a framework for guiding educational practice that provides flexibility, reduces instructional barriers, and maintains high achievement expectations for all students. It also endorses UDL's application to assessment design, literacy programs, and increased access to rigorous learning experiences supported by technology for all students, including students with disabilities and ELs.

Bilingual, special education and UDL policies have their roots in the nation's equal opportunity provisions going as far back as the statement in the Declaration of Independence that pronounced that "all men are created equal."

In conclusion, our country's early days reveal that children with disabilities or those who had difficulty learning were either neglected, locked away, or subjected to abuse and mistreatment with little access to protection under the law. In the late 1800s, special day schools and residential schools were established for children with obvious sensory disabilities, such as blindness, deafness, or physical disabilities. Only the wealthy had access to these programs. After World War II, public schools began to recognize their responsibility to offer education programs to students with disabilities, but it was often provided in a separate site or in segregated, self-contained classes. This situation changed as perspectives on special needs began to advance in the late 1960s and 1970s.

Over the last 240 years, federal policy moved from a stance of condoning—and in some cases, even encouraging discrimination against students with special needs—to protecting their right to a free, appropriate public education (FAPE). No one law or court case established all the rights and benefits that exist today. They developed over time, each adding a new focus or expanded protection to the last. Since federal policy evolved over a long time, equity for people with disabilities and ELs is a relatively recent expectation. At the beginning of the twenty-first century, federal policy recognized UDL as an effective solution for offering accessibility, flexibility, and literacy instruction to all students, including students with disabilities and ELs.

A FINAL WORD

Understanding the evolution of federal policies that today protect students' rights to equity, equal opportunities, and effective services, you can be a successful advocate for all your learners. Finally, the federal policies discussed in this chapter and the instructional guidance offered in the previous chapters bring us back to the main premise of this book: by weaving together the CRT and UDL frameworks into your learning environment design and lesson planning, you will create engaging, meaningful, and culturally responsive learning environments for all your learners, including ELs and CLD students.

REFLECTION QUESTIONS

1. What's surprising to you about the history of disability and bilingual policies?

2. How does federal and state policy impact your learners?

3. To what extent are ELs receiving special education services in your school or district? How appropriate is their education?

4. How can knowing about UDL, special education, and EL policy help you to ensure that your EL students are receiving FAPE?

5. In what way can you be proactive to ensure that your students receive the education to which they are entitled?

EXERCISE YOUR LEARNING: POLICY MATRIX

Select a policy (court case, legislation, policy report) and complete the policy matrix shown here.

POLICY MATRIX

QUESTION	YOUR RESPONSE
What is your policy's official name?	
When was it enacted or decided? (date)	
In a brief sentence or two, report how your selected policy impacts the education of ELs either with or without disabilities. For example, did it grant a civil right or clarify an entitlement?	
Is its impact still evident today? If so, how?	

CHECK-IN: TWO TRUTHS AND A LIE

Read the following statements. Determine which two are true and which one is a lie.

1. The U.S. Constitution is the basis for providing equal protection under the law for all individuals, including students with disabilities and ELs.

2. Universal Design for Learning (UDL) is not mentioned in federal legislation.

3. Federal legislation guarantees all students with disabilities and ELs the right to a free, appropriate public education (FAPE).

   Answer is at the end of the Glossary.

GLOSSARY

A

ACCESS
How a learner first processes information or content (i.e., digital media, visual media, printed text, audio, or touch (Bray & McClaskey, 2015).

ACCOMMODATIONS
Strategies, services, or supports that are provided to the student in curriculum, instruction, and assessment that do not change the content of the materials and the level of the playing field for a student with a disability (e.g., extended time, sign language interpreter) (Johnes, 2006).

ADAPTED
Changes in materials, usually by simplifying language without watering down the content (adapted from Haynes & Zacarian, 2010).

ASSISTIVE TECHNOLOGY (AT) DEVICE
"Any item, piece of equipment, or product system, whether acquired commercially off the shelf, modified or customized that is used to increase, maintain, or improve functional capabilities of a child with a disability" (20 U.S.C. 1401; Johnes, 2006).

B

BASIC INTERPERSONAL COMMUNICATION SKILLS (BICS)
The skills required for verbal face-to-face social communication (Haynes & Zacarian, 2010).

C

CIVIL RIGHT
A personal right guaranteed by the U.S. Constitution, a state constitution, or a federal or state law (Osborne & Russo, 2014).

COGNITIVE ACADEMIC LANGUAGE PROFICIENCY (CALP)
The academic language of the content of the classroom, which takes 4–10 years to develop (Haynes & Zacarian, 2010).

COLLABORATION
The process of working together in a partnership with other individuals with whom you have a common purpose of assisting a student (Johnes, 2006).

CULTURE
Collectively, the beliefs, customs, practices, and social behavior of a particular group of people (inclusive of age, gender, race, ethnicity, culture, disability or sexual preference) (Cole, 2008).

D

DOMINANCE/DOMINANT LANGUAGE
Having greater grammatical proficiency, more vocabulary, and greater fluency in one language than in another. Using one language more than another (Paradis et al., 2011).

DUAL/SECOND-LANGUAGE LEARNERS
Children who begin to learn an additional language after the first language is established (after age 3 years) (Paradis et al., 2011).

E

ENGLISH FOR SPEAKERS OF OTHER LANGUAGES (ESOL)
K–12 programs of English language instruction for non-English speakers; also known as English as a second language (ESL) (adapted from Haynes & Zacarian, 2010).

ENGLISH LANGUAGE LEARNERS (ELS)

Students in the United States and Canada who are learning English, the majority language. This is the term most commonly used in current federal legislation. Previously referred to as limited English proficient (LEP). Similar terms include English as a second language (ESL) learners, English as an additional language (EAL) learners, and English learners (ELs) (Paradis et al., 2011).

ENGLISH-ONLY PROGRAMS

K–12 programs in the United States that only use English as the language of instruction in general education classrooms. English as a second language (ESL) services may be provided by ESL specialists (Paradis et al., 2011).

F

FIRST LANGUAGE (L1)

The first or native language, usually spoken in the home. Also known as heritage language or primary language (adapted from Haynes & Zacarian, 2010).

I

INDIVIDUALIZED EDUCATION PROGRAM (IEP)

A written statement for each child with a disability that is developed, reviewed, and revised in an annual meeting. An IEP includes a statement of present level of academic achievement and functional performance, measurable annual goals, how progress toward those goals with be measured, and the special education and related services and supplementary aids and services to be provided to the student (adapted from Johnes, 2006).

L

LANGUAGE APTITUDE

Ability or potential that an individual has for learning language (Paradis et al., 2011).

LANGUAGE SOCIALIZATION
Process of cultural socialization through language; process of cultural patterning that teaches children how and with whom to use language (Paradis et al., 2011).

N

NONDOMINANT LANGUAGE
The language than is less proficient for a bilingual learner (Paradis et al., 2011).

NONVERBAL PERIOD
Stage that occurs early in the acquisition of a second language during which children do not speak or speak very little when in the presence of speakers of that second language. They may communicate through nonverbal gestures but produce very few or no spoken language (Paradis et al., 2011).

R

READINESS
Developmental point at which a person has the capacity and willingness to engage in a particular activity, such as learning (Bray & McClaskey, 2015).

S

SELF-REGULATION
Learners are concerned with what they need to do to generate and sustain their engagement and learning (Bray & McClaskey, 2015).

SEMANTIC WEBBING
Semantic webbing is a method that students can use to activate prior knowledge and organize information as part of the prewriting process. Usually, a graphic organizer is used to help students develop a visual that organizes and outlines their ideas. Adapted from Renico (n.d.).

SHELTERED ENGLISH IMMERSION (SEI)
The process of simplifying the language of instruction to teach content area material (Haynes & Zacarian, 2010).

SHELTERED INSTRUCTION OBSERVATION PROTOCOL (SIOP)
A strategy for describing instructional practices that help teachers make content accessible to ELs (Haynes & Zacarian, 2010).

SPECIAL EDUCATION
Instruction specifically designed to meet the unique needs of a student with disabilities (Osborne & Russo, 2014).

STEREOTYPE THREAT
A phenomenon experienced by members of groups that have been stigmatized as inferior in academics resulting from anxiety over confirming negative stereotypes (American Psychological Association, July 15, 2006).

V

VARIABILITY
The degree of difference between learners. No one is average (Bray & McClaskey, 2015).

Z

ZONE OF PROXIMAL DEVELOPMENT (ZPD)
Based on Vygotsky's theory of learning, ZPD is the distance between a learner's ability to perform a task with adult guidance and/or peer collaboration and the learner's ability to perform the task independently. Learning occurs in this zone (Bray & McClaskey, 2015).

Check-In: Two Truths and a Lie answer is #1 and #3 are true. #2 is not.

REFERENCES

Abedi, J. (2010). *Performance assessments for English language learners*. Stanford, CA: Stanford University, Stanford Center for Opportunity Policy in Education.

Albus, D. A., & Thurlow, M. L. (2007). English language learners with disabilities in state English language proficiency assessments: A review of state accommodation policies (Synthesis Report 66). Minneapolis, MN: University of Minnesota, National Center on Educational Outcomes.

Allen, R. (2012, August). Support struggling students with academic rigor: A conversation with author and educator Robyn Jackson. *Teaching Financial Literacy 54*(8), 3–5. Retrieved from *www.ascd.org/publications/newsletters/education-update/aug12/vol54/num08/Support-Struggling-Students-with-Academic-Rigor.aspx* (accessed June 16, 2017).

American Psychological Association. (2006, July 15). What is stereotype threat? What is psychology? Retrieved from *www.whatispsychology.biz/about-stereotype-threat-define* (accessed June 25, 2017).

Au, W. (2014). *Rethinking multicultural education: Teaching for racial and cultural justice* (2nd ed.). Milwaukee, WI: Rethinking Schools, Ltd.

Baca, L. M., & Cervantes, H. T. (2004). *The bilingual special education interface*. Upper Saddle River, NJ: Pearson.

Beck, I. L., McKeown, M. G., & Kucan, L. (2002). *Bringing words to life*. New York: The Guilford Press.

Bohanon, H., Fenning, P., Carney, K. L., Minnis-Kim, M. J., Anderson-Harriss, S., Moroz, K. B., Hicks, K. J., Kasper, B. B., Culos, C., Sailor, W., & Pigott, T. D. (2006). Schoolwide application of positive behavior support in an urban high school: A case study. *Journal of Positive Behavior Interventions 8*(3), 131–145.

Braun, R. L., & Simpson, W. R. (2004). The pause method in undergraduate auditing: An analysis of student assessments and relative effectiveness. *Advances in Accounting Education Teaching and Curriculum Innovations 6*, 69–85.

Bray, B., & McClaskey, K. (2015). *Make learning personal: The what, who, wow, where, and why.* Thousand Oaks, CA: Corwin Press.

Bronfenbrenner, U. (1981). *The ecology of human development: Experiments by nature and design.* Cambridge, MA: Harvard University Press.

Brookhart, S. (2013). *How to create and use rubrics for formative assessment and grading.* Alexandria, VA: Association for Supervision and Curriculum Development.

Brown, D. F. (2003). Urban teachers' use of culturally responsive management strategies. *Theory into Practice 42*(4), 277–282.

Brown University (2017). Culturally Responsive Teaching. Retrieved from *https://www.brown.edu/academics/education-alliance/teaching-diverse-learners/strategies-O/culturally-responsive-teaching-O* (accessed June 16, 2017).

Bruce, A., Getch, Y., & Ziomek-Daigle, J. (2009). Closing the gap: A group counseling approach to improve test performance of African-American students. *Professional School Counseling 12*(6), 450–457.

CAST. (2014). UDL Guidelines. Wakefield, MA: CAST, Inc.

Center for Advanced Research on Language Acquisition (2009). What is culture? Minneapolis, MN: Author, University of Minnesota.

Retrieved from *http://carla.umn.edu/culture/definitions.html* (accessed June 16, 2017).

Center on the Developing Child at Harvard University. (2011). Building the brain's "Air Traffic Control" system: How early experiences shape the development of executive function (Working Paper No. 11). Cambridge, MA: Author. Retrieved from *http://developingchild.harvard.edu/wp-content/uploads/2011/05/How-Early-Experiences-Shape-the-Development-of-Executive-Function.pdf* (accessed June 16, 2017).

Checkley, K. (1995). Balancing student choice and curriculum goals. *Student-Directed Learning 37*(9). Retrieved from *www.ascd.org/publications/newsletters/education_update/dec95/vol37/num09/Student-Directed_Learning.aspx* (accessed June 16, 2017).

Chita-Tegmark, M., Gravel, J. W., Serpa, M. D. B., Domings, Y., and Rose, D. H. (2012). Using the Universal Design for Learning framework to support culturally diverse learners. *Journal of Education 192*(1), 17–22.

Center for International Competence. (2017). Typical examples of cultural differences. Fribourg, Switzerland: Author. Retrieved from *www.cicb.net/en/home/examples* (accessed June 16, 2017).

Cole, R. W. (2008). *Educating everybody's children: Diverse teaching strategies for diverse learners.* Alexandria, VA: Association for Curriculum and Supervision Development.

Coles-Ritchie, M., & Smith, R. R. (2017). Taking the risk to engage in race talk: professional development in elementary schools. *International Journal of Inclusive Education 21*(2), 172–186.

Cummins, J. (1984). *Bilingualism and special education.* Bristol, UK: Multilingual Matters.

DiAngelo, R., & Sensoy, O. (2010). "OK, I get it! Now tell me how to do it!" Why we can't just tell you how to do critical multicultural education. *Multicultural Perspectives 12*(2), 97–102.

Dimitriadis, G., & Kamberelis, G. (2006). *Theory for education*. New York: Taylor & Francis.

Durey, E. (2010). Student diversity is up but teachers are mostly white. Retrieved from *https://aacte.org/news-room/aacte-in-the-news/347-student-diversity-is-up-but-teachers-are-mostly-white* (accessed June 16, 2017).

Drake, S. M., & Burns, R. C. (2004). *Meeting standards through integrated curriculum*. Alexandria, VA: Association for Supervision and Curriculum Development.

Dweck, C. (2016, January 11). Recognizing and overcoming false growth mindset. Edutopia. Retrieved from *https://www.edutopia.org/blog/recognizing-overcoming-false-growth-mindset-carol-dweck* (accessed June 16, 2017).

Dweck, C. S. (2006). *Mindset: The new psychology of success*. New York: Random House.

Early, D. M., Rogge, R. D., & Deci, E. L. (2014). Engagement, alignment, and rigor as vital signs of high-quality instruction: A classroom visit protocol for instructional improvement and research. *The High School Journal* 97(4), 219–239.

Echevarria, J., Vogt, M., & Short, D.J. (2017). *Making content comprehensible for English learners: The SIOP Model* (5th ed.). London, England: Pearson.

Ee, J. (2013). "He's an idiot!" Experiences of international students in the United States. *Journal of International Students* 3(1), 72–77.

Ferlazzo, L. (2015). "Culturally Responsive Teaching": An interview with Zaretta Hammond. Retrieved from *http://blogs.edweek.org/teachers/classroom_qa_with_larry_ferlazzo/2015/07/culturally_responsive_teaching_an_interview_with_zaretta_hammond.html* (accessed June 16, 2017).

Fisher, D. (2008). Effective use of the Gradual Release of Responsibility Model. Retrieved from *https://www.mheonline.com/_treasures/pdf/douglas_fisher.pdf* (accessed June 16, 2017).

Galdi, S., Cadinu, M., & Tomasetto, C. (2014). The roots of stereotype threat: When automatic associations disrupt girls' math performance. *Child Development 85*(1), 250–263.

Ganley, C. M., Mingle, L. A., Ryan, A. M., Ryan, K., Vasilyeva, M., & Perry, M. (2013). An examination of stereotype threat effects on girls' mathematics performance. *Developmental Psychology 49*(10), 1886–1897.

Gay, G. (2010). *Culturally Responsive Teaching: Theory, research, and practice.* New York: Teachers College Press.

Gay, G. (2013). Teaching to and through cultural diversity. *Curriculum Inquiry 43*(1), 48–70.

Gee, J. P. (1996). *Social linguistics and literacies: Ideology in discourses.* London, England: Falmer Press.

Giroux, H., & Penna, A. (1979). Social education in the classroom: The dynamics of the hidden curriculum. *Theory and Research in Social Education 7*(1), 21–42.

González, N., Moll, L. C., & Amanti, C. (Eds). (2005). *Funds of knowledge: Theorizing practices in households, communities and classrooms.* Mahwah, NJ: Lawrence Erlbaum.

Greenstein, L. (2010). *What teachers really need to know about formative assessment.* Alexandria, VA: Association for Supervision and Curriculum Development.

Guskey, T. (2000) *Evaluating Professional Development.* Thousand Oaks, CA: Corwin Press, Inc.

Hale, J. E. (1994). *Unbrink the fire: Visions for the education of African American children.* Baltimore, MD: The John Hopkins University Press.

Halliday, M. A. K., & Hasan, R., (1985). *Language, context, and text: Aspects of language in a social semiotic perspective.* Geelong, Australia: Deakin University Press.

Hammond, Z. (2015). *Culturally Responsive Teaching & the brain: Promoting authentic engagement and rigor among culturally and linguistically diverse students.* Thousand Oaks, CA: Corwin.

Hanley, M. S., & Noblit, G. W. (2009). Cultural responsiveness, racial identity and academic success: A review of literature. The Heinz Endowments. Retrieved from *www.heinz.org/UserFiles/Library/Culture-Report_FINAL.pdf* (accessed June 16, 2017).

Hattie, J. (2003, October). Teachers make a difference: What is the research evidence? Australian Council on Educational Research Annual Conference on: Building Teacher Quality. Retrieved from *www.educationalleaders.govt.nz/Pedagogy-and-assessment/Building-effective-learning-environments/Teachers-Make-a-Difference-What-is-the-Research-Evidence* (accessed June 16, 2017).

Hattie, J. (2009). *Visible learning: A synthesis of over 800 meta-analyses related to achievement.* New York: Routledge.

Haynes, J. (n.d.). Language acquisition vs. language learning. Retrieved from *www.everythingesl.net/inservices/language_acquisiti_vs_language_02033.php* (accessed June 25, 2017).

Haynes, J., & Zacarian, D. (2010). *Teaching English language learners across the content areas.* Alexandria, VA: ASCD,

Hedges, H. (2012). Teachers' funds of knowledge: A challenge to evidence-based practice. *Teachers and Teaching: Theory and Practice 18*(1), 7–24.

Henfield, M. S. (2011). Black male adolescents navigating microaggressions in a traditionally white middle school: A qualitative study. *Journal of Multicultural Counseling and Development 39*(2), 141–156.

Higher Education Opportunity Act, Pub. L. No. 110-315, 20 U.S.C., § 103, 122 Stat. 3078 (2008). Retrieved from *www.gpo.gov/*

fdsys/pkg/PLAW-110publ315/pdf/PLAW-110publ315.pdf (accessed June 16, 2017).

Hill, J. D., & Miller, K. B. (2013). *Classroom instruction that works with English language learners.* Alexandria, VA: Association for Supervision and Curriculum Development.

Hogg, L. (2011). Funds of knowledge: An investigation of coherence within the literature. *Teaching and Teacher Education, 27,* 666–677.

Hollins, E. R. (1996). *Culture in school learning: Revealing the deep meaning.* Mahwah, NJ: Lawrence Erlbaum Associates.

hooks, b. 1994. *Teaching to transgress: Education as the practice of freedom.* New York: Routledge.

Immordino-Yang, M. H, & Damasio, A. (2007). We feel, therefore we learn: The relevance of affective and social neuroscience to education. *International Mind, Brain, and Education Society 1,* 3–10.

Jackson, P. (1968). *Life in classrooms.* New York: Holt, Rinehart, and Winston.

Johnes, G. (2006). Didacticism and educational outcomes. *Educational Research and Reviews 1*(2), 23–29.

Jordan, C. (1995). Creating cultures of schooling: Historical and conceptual background of the KEEP/Rough Rock collaboration. *The Bilingual Research Journal 19*(1), 83–100.

King, A. (1993). From sage on the stage to guide on the side. *College Teaching 4*(1), 30–35.

Klingner, J. & Eppolito, A. (2014). *English language learners: Differentiating between language acquisition and learning disabilities.* Arlington, VA: Council for Exceptional Children.

Kozleski, E. B. (2008). Culturally Responsive Teaching matters! Retrieved from *www.equityallianceatasu.org/sites/default/files/ Website_files/CulturallyResponsiveTeaching-Matters.pdf* (accessed June 16, 2017).

LaBerge, D., & Samuels, S. J. (1974). Toward a theory of automatic information process in reading. *Cognitive Psychology 6*, 293–323.

Ladson-Billings, G. (2001). *Crossing over to Canaan: The journey of new teachers in diverse classrooms.* Hoboken, NJ: John Wiley & Sons, Inc.

Ladson-Billings, G. (2009). *The dreamkeepers: Successful teaching for African-American students.* Hoboken, NJ: John Wiley & Sons, Inc.

Langhout R. D., & Mitchell, C. A. (2008). Engaging contexts: Drawing the link between student and teacher experiences of the hidden curriculum. *Journal of Community & Applied Social Psychology 18*(6), 593–614.

Lee, C. D. (2001). Is October Brown Chinese? A cultural modeling activity system for underachieving students. *American Educational Research Journal, 38*(1), 97–141.

Lenski, S., & Verbruggen, F. (2010). *Writing instruction and assessment for English language learners K–8.* New York, NY: Guilford Press.

Lopez, J. K. (n.d.). Funds of knowledge. Retrieved from *www.learnnc. org/lp/pages/939* (accessed June 16, 2017).

Markos, A., & Himmel, J. (2016). *Using sheltered instruction to support English learners.* Washington, DC: Center for Applied Linguistics.

Marzano, R. J., Pickering, D. J., & Pollack, J. E. (2001). *Classroom instruction that works.* Alexandria, VA: Association for Supervision and Curriculum Development.

Marzano, R., Marzano, J., and Pickering, D. (2003). *Classroom management that works: Research based strategies for every teacher.* Alexandria, VA: Association for Supervision and Curriculum Development.

Mattia, P. R., Wagle, A. T., & Williams, J. M. (2010). An often-neglected issue in consideration of gifted African American millennial students: Implications for school planning and policy. *Gifted Child Today Magazine* 32(2), 26–31.

McIntosh, K., Girvan, E. J., Horner, R., & Smolkowski, K. (2014). Education not incarceration: A conceptual model for reducing racial and ethnic disproportionality in school discipline. *Journal for Applied Research on Children: Informing Policy for Children at Risk,* 5(2), 1–22.

Metropolitan Center for Urban Education, New York University. (2008). Culturally responsive classroom management strategies. Retrieved from *http://steinhardt.nyu.edu/scmsAdmin/uploads/005/121/ Culturally%20Responsive%20Classroom%20Mgmt%20Strat2.pdf* (accessed June 16, 2017).

Meacham, M. (2014, October). All learning is emotional. Learning to Go. Retrieved from *https://learningtogo.info/2014/10/16/all-learning-is-emotional/* (accessed June 16, 2017).

Meyer, A., Rose, D. H., & Gordon, D. (2014). *Universal Design for Learning: Theory and practice.* Wakefield, MA: CAST Professional Publishing.

Moll, L., Amanti, C., Neff, D. & González, N. (1992). Funds of knowledge for teaching: Using a qualitative approach to connect homes and classrooms. *Theory Into Practice* 31(2), 132–141.

National Center for Education Statistics. (2016). *Digest of education statistics.* Washington, DC: U.S. Department of Education. Retrieved from *https://nces.ed.gov/programs/digest/*

National Center for Research on Cultural Diversity and Second Language Learning. (1992, December). Myths and misconceptions about second language learning. *CAL Digest.* Retrieved from *www. ericdigests.org/1992-1/myths.htm* (accessed June 16, 2017).

Nelson, L. L. (2014). *Design and deliver: Planning and teaching using Universal Design for Learning.* Baltimore, MD: Paul H. Brookes Publishing.

New London Group (1996). A pedagogy of multiliteracies: Designing social futures. *Harvard Educational Review 66*(1), 60–92.

Nieto, S. (1996). *Affirming diversity: The sociopolitical context of multicultural education* (2nd ed.). White Plains, NY: Longman.

Nisbett, R. E., Peng, K., Choi, I., & Norenzayan, A. (2001). Culture and systems of thoughts: Holistic versus analytic cognition. *Psychological Review 108*(2), 291–310.

Nuri-Robins, K. J., Lindsey, D. B., Lindsey, R. B., & Terrell, R. D. (2012). *Culturally proficient instruction: A guide for people who teach.* Thousand Oaks, CA: Corwin Press.

Olmedo, I. M. (1997). Family oral histories for multicultural curriculum perspectives. *Urban Education, 32,* 45–62.

Orosco, M. J., & O'Connor, R. (2011). Cultural aspects of teaching reading with Latino English language learners. In R. O'Connor & P. Vadasy (Eds.), *Handbook of reading interventions* (pp. 356–379). New York: Guilford.

Osborne, A. G., & Russo, C. J. (2014). *Special education and the law: A guide for practitioners.* Thousand Oaks, CA: Corwin Press.

Paradis, J., Genesee, F., & Crago, M. B. (2011). *Dual language development and disorders.* Baltimore, MD: Paul Brookes Publishing.

Pearson, P. D., & Gallagher, M. C. (1983). The instruction of reading comprehension. *Contemporary Educational Psychology 8*(3), 317–344.

Persell, C. H. (1977). *Education and inequality: The roots and results of stratification in America's schools.* New York: The Free Press.

Picho, K. (2016). The psychosocial experience of high school girls highly susceptible to stereotype threat: A phenomenological study. *Journal of Educational Research 109*(6), 608–623.

Popham, W. J., & Lindheim, E. (1980). The practical side of criterion-referenced test development. *NCME Measurement in Education* *10*(4), 1–8.

Project Implicit. (2011). Retrieved from *https://implicit.harvard.edu/implicit/* (accessed June 16, 2017).

Ralabate, P. K. (2016). *Your UDL lesson planner: The step-by-step guide to teaching all learners.* Baltimore, MD: Paul H. Brookes Publishing Co.

Renico, L. (n.d.). How to do semantic webbing. Retrieved from *http://classroom.synonym.com/do-semantic-webbing-8665670.html* (accessed June 26, 2017).

Rimm-Kaufman, S., & Sandilos, L. (n.d.). Improving students' relationships with teachers to provide essential supports for learning. Retrieved from *www.apa.org/education/k12/relationships.aspx* (accessed June 16, 2017).

Rios, F. A. (Ed.). (1996). *Teacher thinking in cultural contexts.* New York: State University of New York Press.

Rodríguez, B. A. (2014). The threat of living up to expectations: Analyzing the performance of Hispanic students on standardized exams. *Journal of Hispanic Higher Education* *13*(3), 191–205.

Rose, D. H., & Meyer, A. (2002). *Teaching every student in the digital age: Universal design for learning.* Alexandria, VA: Association for Supervision and Curriculum Development.

Rose, L. T., Rouhani, P., & Fischer, K. W. (2013). The science of the individual. *Mind, Brain, and Education, 7*(3), 152–158.

Rudner, L., & Shafer, W. (2002). *What teachers need to know about assessment.* Washington, DC: National Education Association.

Sansone, C., & Smith, J. L. (2000). Interest and self-regulation: The relation between having to and wanting to. In C. Sansone & J. M. Harackiewicz (Eds.), *Intrinsic and extrinsic motivation: The search for optimal motivation and performance* (pp. 341–372). San Diego, CA: Academic Press.

Sansone, C., & Thoman, D. B. (2005). Interest as the missing motivator in self-regulation. *European Psychologist 10*(3), 175–186.

Short, D. J., & Fitzsimmons, S. (2007). *Double the work: Challenges and solutions to acquiring language and academic literacy for adolescent English language learners.* New York: Carnegie Corporation.

Singleton, G. E., & Linton, C. (2006). *Courageous conversations about race: A field guide to achieving equity in schools.* Newbury Park, CA: Corwin Press.

Smolkowski, K., Girvan, E. J., McIntosh, K., Nese, R. N. T., & Horner, R. (2016). Vulnerable decision points for disproportionate office discipline referrals: Comparisons of discipline for African American and White elementary school students. *Behavioral Disorders 41*(4), 178–195.

Staats, C. (2016). Understanding implicit bias. *Education Digest, 1,* 29–38.

Subero, D., Vila, I., & Esteban-Guitart, M. (2015). Some contemporary forms of the funds of knowledge approach: Developing culturally responsive pedagogy for social justice. *International Journal of Educational Psychology, 4*(1), 33–53. doi: 10.4471/ijep.2015.02

Sue, D. W., Capodilupo, C. M., Torino, G. C., Bucceri, J. M., Holder, A. M. B., Nadal, K. L., & Esquilin, M. (2007). Racial microaggressions in everyday life: Implications for clinical practice. *American Psychologist 64*(2), 271–286.

Tateishi, C. A. (2014). *Why are all the Asian American kids silent in class?* In W. Au (Ed.). Rethinking Multicultural Education: Teaching for racial and cultural justice (149-158). Milwaukee, WI: Rethinking Schools.

Tatum, B. D. (1997). *Why are all the black kids sitting together in the cafeteria: And other conversations about race.* New York: Basic Books.

Taylor, V. J., & Walton, G. M. (2011). Stereotype threat undermines learning. *Personality and Social Psychology Bulletin* 37(8), 1055–1067.

Thoman, D. B., Smith, J. L., Brown, E. R., Chase, J., & Lee, J. Y. K. (2013). Beyond performance: A motivational experiences model of stereotype threat. *Educational Psychology Review 25*, 211–243. doi: 10.1007/s10648-013-9219-1.

Thomas, W. P., & Collier, V. P. (2003). The multiple benefits of dual language. *Educational Leadership 61*(2), 61–64.

Torff, B. (2003). Developmental changes in teachers' use of higher order thinking and content knowledge. *Journal of Educational Psychology 95*(3), 563–569.

Ukpokodu, O. (2011). How do I teach mathematics in a culturally responsive way? Identifying empowering teaching practices. *Multicultural Education 18*(3), 47–56.

Ung, S. (2015). Integrating culture into psychological research. *Association for Psychological Science Observer 28*, 37–38.

U.S. Census. (2013). 2009–2013 American Community Survey. Retrieved from *https://www.census.gov/data/tables/2013/demo/2009-2013-lang-tables.html* (accessed June 16, 2017)

U.S. Department of Education. (2007). 25 year history of IDEA. Washington, DC: Author. Retrieved from *http://www2.ed.gov/policy/speced/leg/idea/history.html* (accessed June 16, 2017).

van den Bergh, L., Denessen, E., Hornstra, L., Voeten, M., & Holland, R. W. (2010). The implicit prejudiced attitudes of teachers. *American Educational Research Journal 47*(2), 497–527.

Vélez-Ibáñez, C., & Greenberg, J. (1992). Formation and transformation of funds of knowledge among U.S. Mexican households. *Anthropology and Education Quarterly 23*, 313–335.

Viadero, D. (2007). Experiments aim to ease effects of 'stereotype threat.' *Education Week 27*(9), 10–14.

Vygotsky, L. S. (1962). *Thought and language*. Cambridge MA: MIT Press.

Vygotsky, L. S. (1978). *Mind in society*. Cambridge, MA: Harvard University Press.

Waitoller, F. R., & Thorius, K. J. (2016). Cross-pollinating culturally sustaining pedagogy and Universal Design for Learning: Toward an inclusive pedagogy that accounts for dis/ability. *Harvard Educational Review 86*(3), 366–389.

Weinstein C., Tomlinson-Clarke S., & Curran M. (2004). Toward a conception of culturally responsive classroom management. *Journal of Teacher Education 55*(1), 25–38.

WIDA Consortium. (2007). *Understanding the WIDA English language proficiency standards: A resource guide* (3rd. ed.). Madison, WI: Wisconsin Center for Education Research (WCER).

WIDA Consortium. (2012). Can-do descriptors for the levels of English language proficiency. Retrieved from *http://opi.mt.gov/PDF/Assessment/ELP/12WIDA-Can-Do.pdf* (accessed June 16, 2017).

WIDA Consortium. (2014). *2012 Amplification of the English language development standards, kindergarten–grade 12*. Madison, WI: Board of Regents of the University of Wisconsin System.

Williamson, R., & Blackburn, B. R. (2010). 4 myths about rigor in the classroom. Eye on Education. Larchmont, NY. Retrieved from *http://static.pdesas.org/content/documents/M1-Slide_21_4_Myths_of_Rigor.pdf* (accessed June 16, 2017).

Willis, J. (2012). Bilingual brains—Smarter & faster. *Psychology Today*. Retrieved from *https://www.psychologytoday.com/blog/radical-teaching/201211/bilingual-brains-smarter-faster* (accessed June 16, 2017).

Wolf, E. (1966). *Peasants*. Englewood Cliffs, NJ: Prentice-Hall.

Wood, D., Bruner, J., and Ross, G. (1976). The role of tutoring in problem solving. *Journal of Child Psychology and Child Psychiatry 17*, 89–100.

Wren, D. J. (1999). School culture: Exploring the hidden curriculum. *Adolescence 34*(135), 593–597.

Zion, S., & Kozleski, E. (2005). Understanding culture. OnPoint. Tempe, AZ: National Institute for Urban School Improvement. Retrieved from *http://guide.swiftschools.org/sites/default/files/documents/Understanding_Culture_Part_1.pdf* (accessed June 16, 2017).

INDEX

learning environment
    conversations about race, 72–75
    expert learners, 53–54
    funds of knowledge, 55–61
    hidden barriers, 61–62
    hidden curriculum, 62–65
    implicit bias, 65–68
    microaggressions, 70–72
    overview, 26–28, 30, 52–53
    stereotype threat, 68–70
learning goals
    adding scaffolds for, 38
    communicating, 32
    linking to knowledge, 130
    sharing with families, 143
    SMART, 139–140
learning needs, anticipating, 38
learning networks, 16
Lee (teacher scenario), 161
Leo (teacher scenario), 138–139
Lesson Design
    assessment, 148–153
    choice and challenge, 144–145
    clarifying objectives, 39
    core cognitive demand, 144
    expectations, 142
    flexibility, 141
    language development, 141–142
    learning goals, 139–143
    methods, materials, media,
        153–156
    process, 137
    refining through reflection, 156–159
    reflection worksheet, 160
    rubrics, 153
    scaffolds, 155
    student-centered instruction,
        38–39
    summarizing, 158
    variability, 143–148
linguistic demands, 145–147
listen demand, 145–147
listening and reading, 111
literacy. See multi-literacies
Long-Term EL, 19
LRE (least restrictive environment), 167
Luis (teacher scenario), 101–102
Lydia (teacher scenario), 25–26, 47

M

mastery feedback, 132–134
materials
    contextualizing, 153–156
    culturally responsive, 155
Mathematics, L2 proficiency, 108
media
    contextualizing, 153–156
    culturally responsive, 155
methods, contextualizing, 153–156
Mexican American Legal Defense and
    Education Fund & the NEA, 59
Mia and Manny (teacher scenario), 81–82
microaggressions, 28, 70–72
Mills v. BOE of the District of Columbia
    (1972), 170–171
minority parent and community
    engagement, 59. *See also* students
    of color
Moll, Luis, 57–58
motivated learners, 8, 10
multicultural viewpoints, 41–43
multilingual speakers, 42
multi-literacies, building, 111–112

N

naming pictures, 15
National Center for Education
    Statistics, 60
National Center for Research on
    Cultural Diversity and Second
    Language Learning, 21
National Education Technology Plan
    (2010), 178
NEA (National Education Association),
    58
Neff, Deborah, 57–58
neural pathways and experiences,
    14–15, 22
neural patterns and executive
    functions, 83–84
New London Group, 111
New York University's Metropolitan
    Center for Urban Education, 42
Newcomers, schooling of, 19
No Child Left Behind (2002), 176
nonverbal demand, 145

ABOUT THE AUTHORS

PATTI KELLY RALABATE, EdD, is the author of the bestseller *Your UDL Lesson Planner: The Step-by-Step Guide for Teaching All Learners* (Paul H. Brookes, 2016) and former Director of Implementation at CAST, where she guided a multi-district UDL implementation initiative funded by the Bill & Melinda Gates Foundation. She was the special education expert in the National Education Association's policy and practice department, and an early partner in the National UDL Task Force that successfully brought UDL into federal policy. She has nearly three decades of teaching experience as a speech language pathologist and holds a doctorate in special education from the George Washington University in Washington, DC.

LOUI LORD NELSON, PhD, is an international educational consultant who focuses on Universal Design for Learning. A former special education teacher, Loui provides guidance in UDL to schools, districts, state personnel, and universities across the globe and is the author of the top selling book, *Design and Deliver: Planning and Teaching Using Universal Design for Learning* (Paul H. Brookes, 2014). She also works as the UDL Specialist for the School Wide Integrated Framework for Transformation (SWIFT), a national project that aims to shift American education to truly meet the needs of all learners.